Leaving a restaurant in Chicago's ___ sunny afternoon in 1925, "Bloody" Angelo Genna and three "button men" spied a certain Paul Labriola—a campaign worker for a mayoral candidate Genna disliked intensely.

As Labriola nervously headed across the street, avoiding eye contact with the four men, Genna gave the word. The bright afternoon exploded with a volley of gunfire that shattered Labriola and left him twitching in the gutter.

Picking his teeth, Genna sauntered over to the fallen man. "He ain't done yet," he observed, and then blew a few more holes in Labriola's head. He squinted like a craftsman at his handiwork.

"He's done now," Genna said, nodding. Then the four men strolled to their car and drove calmly away.

RUBOUTS
MOB MURDERS IN AMERICA

RICHARD MONACO
AND
LIONEL BASCOM

AVON BOOKS ◆ NEW YORK

RUBOUTS: MOB MURDERS IN AMERICA is an original publication of Avon Books. This work has never before appeared in book form.

AVON BOOKS
A division of
The Hearst Corporation
1350 Avenue of the Americas
New York, New York 10019

Copyright © 1991 by Holy Grail, Inc.
Cover and text photographs courtesy of AP/Wide World Photos
Published by arrangement with Holy Grail, Inc.
Library of Congress Catalog Card Number: 91-91779
ISBN: 0-380-75938-1

First Avon Books Printing: August 1991

AVON TRADEMARK REG. U.S. PAT. OFF. AND IN OTHER COUNTRIES, MARCA REGISTRADA, HECHO EN U.S.A.

Printed in the U.S.A.

RA   10   9   8   7   6   5   4   3   2   1

Table of Contents

Introduction

AMERICAN crime began to develop serious organization around the time of the Civil War, when the great gangs like the "Dead Rabbits," "Five Points," "Plug Uglies," "Bowery Bhoys," and so on, ruled large sections of New York City. They had their counterparts in other major cities, to be sure, but New York, as ever, set the tone for U.S. crime until the time of Al Capone, who moved the capital, briefly, to Chicago.

Criminals have always killed one another out of greed, revenge, to ensure silence, or in the heat of passion; but the murders in this collection are special in that they were all planned and carried out according to the cold and ruthless calculations of organizations killing as a matter of policy. Here we'll see the classic "hit," "rubout," "clip," "whack," "bump-off," "dump" etc. These are crimes whose victims are mainly criminals—which may be the key to the attraction the public has always had for the sight of the well-dressed gangster stretched out in the gutter like a

1

sack of old clothes near the door of his gleaming Cadillac, or shot to pieces in his barber chair or at his favorite table in a restaurant. Americans have a strange fascination and respect for the gangster (as witness the *kind* of success the *Godfather*-like story has always had here), a sympathy they do not show for rapists, muggers, or others equally violent. This book closely focuses on major hits: the personalities, the circumstances, the details. We have included some near misses, as with Frank Costello, and a mystery or two, like the Jimmy Hoffa case.

Even before movies and television, writings detailing the life and times and passing of gangster-style criminals as a group leaned toward either revulsion or mocking humor, usually because the subjects came from a generally semiliterate class and, as with race humor, were considered "quaint," sort of stupid, and pathetic when trying to ape the manners of "polite" society.

Remember, except for rare movies such as *High Sierra* or books like *The Asphalt Jungle*, the gangster was generally portrayed as either a total psychopath, or a bully who whined for mercy when his rivals or the cops finally caught up with him. He was a product of what they used to call the "slums." If he seemed brave, it was only because he was too dull-witted to know better.

While there are plenty of semiretarded "button men" like the fictional Luca Brasi, there are also the Vito and Michael Corleones. *The Godfather* movie, if not the book, pretty much swept away the old stereotypes from public consciousness while creating new ones—ones not quite as silly or removed from reality.

The truth is, the gangster's life, like that of the combat soldier, has always been rich in irony. Some of the men in this book had the personal force and organizational skills sufficient to have led them (with different origins) to commanding positions in nearly any industry. The irony shows in the macabre humor of Anastasia's last haircut, for instance, or Gallo's uneaten clams, Galante's clenched cigar, and so on.

In this book, we hope we have looked past the violent splash of death to some of the real passions, motives, drives, and aspirations of the men who have helped shape history's dark side in our time.

Chapter 1
Your Hit Parade—1929

Selections from a year rich in drama and death

It was late in June 1929 when the Manhattan police got a tip that a well-known gangster was found dying outside a cemetery in Flushing, Queens. Officers sped across the Fifty-Ninth Street bridge. Sprawled bleeding on the ground was Broadway racketeer Frank Marlow.

The clean shot in the back of his head told investigators everything they needed to know. The Marlow killing was a professional hit. Street stoolies confirmed as much when they were hauled in for questioning. The scuttlebutt was that Marlow had tried to expand his gambling interests, encroaching on hostile turf.

The cops said they knew who the hitter was. Two weeks later they had rounded up several material witnesses, including Boston Louie, whose real name was Edward Lewis, and Mary Selden, known around town as Mickey, a show girl at the Rendezvous Club. Marlow owned a piece of the club. The police also picked up former middleweight boxing champ Johnny Wilson, and Ignatius Coppa, owner of La Tavernelle on West

Fifty-Second Street, where Marlow had his last supper. All they could find out was that Marlow got into his car near the restaurant and was found dying forty-five minutes later in Queens.

Investigators thought that one of their suspects—maybe all of them—knew the whole story but just wasn't talking. They were hauled before a judge, who ordered the whole crowd jailed as material witnesses and held each one on $50,000 bail. Meanwhile, investigators dispatched two detectives to Boston, but would not say exactly who or what they hoped to find there.

If the killing had been an isolated incident in New York, it might have been national news. However, it came at the tail-end of the so-called "Roaring Twenties," a wild and prosperous time in American history, especially for mobsters willing to flaunt the law to make a buck.

In 1926, Dion O'Banion, a florist/bootlegger/gang-leader, who was Al Capone's most threatening competitor, was shot to death in his flower shop. O'Banion's murder spurred a new twist to gang warfare in Chicago. After the funeral, eight touring cars raced down Cicero Street in broad daylight, spraying machine gun fire at Capone's headquarters in the Hawthorne Hotel. Incredibly, casualties were light, but subsequent retaliations left a trail of dead gangsters all over the city. The climax to these brazen daytime assaults came on St. Valentine's Day, 1929, when seven members of O'Banion's gang were lined up against a wall and brutally machine-gunned by Capone's men in the S.M.C. Cartage Company garage on North Clark Street.

Gangland violence was closely tied to bootlegging, both in the United States and Canada, and authorites found themselves linking bizarre killings in Chicago to booze shipments from Canada. A body dumped outside a cemetery in Queens was somehow linked to a payroll heist across the river in New Jersey. It wasn't strange that New York cops would seek suspects as far away as Boston in the Marlow case, not in 1929.

In police stations around the country, cops routinely questioned suspects sporting colorful nicknames like "Scarface," "Bugsy," and "Mad Dog." While cops everywhere were trying to keep working stiffs from having a beer because of Prohibition laws, mobsters who made their fortunes manufacturing or importing booze were blowing each other away in private wars. These crimes, random and swift, kept law-enforcement authorities scurrying for sparse clues.

There was a flurry of police activity after the Marlow killing. Among many others, the cops hauled in Brooklyn racketeer Little Augie Pisano, whose real name was Tony Corofano, and put him under the hot lamp. Carofano, the newly acclaimed leader of a beer running crew, sweated profusely but said nothing.

The word on the street was that Carofano succeeded the late Frankie Yale, who had recently been killed. The cops kept bringing Little Augie downtown to get him to open up, but they got nowhere. Insiders at the cop shop said they hoped to link the Marlow and Yale killings to Alphonse "Scarface" Capone, the Chicago ganglord. Capone was presently in a Philadelphia jail for possession of an illegal gun.

If Capone was involved, which seemed highly possible, nobody was talking. A deep silence surrounded Marlow's death and neither threats nor rewards worked. The only tangible clues the police had, even two weeks into the investigation, were the slugs taken out of Marlow's skull and a pistol found in the trunk of a car.

The cops also raided an apartment in the Sunnyside section of Long Island City, where two of the witnesses had barricaded themselves.

The raid was tense and dramatic, and could have been a scene from *The Untouchables*. Patrol cars blocked off either end of the street in Long Island City, just across the river from Manhattan. Inside were Daniel Gresse, sometimes known as David Gresse, and Nicholas McDermott, two tough boys with long police records. Both had been seen near the cemetery where Marlow's bullet-riddled body was found.

The cops expected a shootout. A witness had seen Gresse and McDermott speeding in the vicinity of the cemetery minutes after Marlow's body was thrown from a moving car just outside the cemetery gates. Their car fit the description of the sedan Marlow had been seen entering outside the restaurant. The apartment houses where Gresse and McDermott and a kid named James Graham, just eighteen years old, were holed up was just ten minutes from the cemetery.

Detectives cautiously approached the apartment and banged on the door. They announced themselves and were let right in. The three men inside had been expecting trouble of another kind.

The police found enough weapons to fend off an army, and a pair of field glasses near a window overlooking the street. These guys were ready for a war.

Gresse produced $20,000 in cash and offered to bribe the detectives into letting him go. He knew he was about to take a hard fall this time. The Feds would be happy to know he had been taken into police custody. Gresse was wanted in New Jersey for killing two men in 1926 during the brazen holdup of a U.S. Post Office truck. Gresse and McDermott were also wanted in connection with shooting a cop and a bank guard during a payroll holdup at the Bell Telephone Laboratories. It had been a cold-blooded killing.

"We expect more arrests very soon," the police commissioner told the pack of reporters and photographers who had descended on the scene. "They will probably be men of the same desperate type as Gresse and McDermott," the commissioner was quoted as saying in one newspaper account.

"We have definitely established that Marlow was killed by rivals upset because he was pushing his racketeering activities into areas that belong to other groups." Ballistics experts were testing the slugs taken from Marlow to determine if any of them had been fired from the recovered weapons. After investigators got Gresse downtown and grilled him for hours, they threatened to pin the whole thing on him unless he started talking. It was a futile threat.

"Marlow's secret will burn with me," Gresse said fiercely.

The police, who tried to sweat out confessions or get bits and pieces of information from the others they were holding, were met with what the press described as "glum stares of injured innocence." It was a sign of the times. About the only thing that was certain was the fact that Marlow had been lured to his death by known associates. That piece of information had been confirmed by Humbert Fugasy, a Brooklyn sportsman and boxing promoter who voluntarily told police what he knew about Marlow's murder.

Fugasy said Marlow got a phone call shortly before he left Le Tavernelle. Fugasy was in the restaurant, and had stopped at Marlow's table to talk about managing their respective prize-fighters. Friends who had dined with Marlow denied he had been called to the phone, but Ignatius Coppa, owner of the place, said that he personally told Marlow about the call and watched as Marlow talked to an unidentified caller.

A two-bit Coney Island dancer known only as Mary told the cops she saw Marlow enter a sedan outside the restaurant with an unidentified companion and drive off.

"I believe this companion actually engineered the killing on behalf of himself and friendly interests who wanted to remove Marlow from competition," said the police commissioner. He then gave reporters the following details:

"We are not very far away from a solution of the murder. We have all the material ends and are working now on details," the police commissioner said. Despite prompting from the reporters surrounding him, the commissioner refused to speculate on when an arrest in the case would be made, or who their prime suspects might be. He would only say that Gresse and McDermott were closely connected to the killing and "knew all about it." Both men would only be held as material witnesses, however, not as suspects for the time being.

A muckraking reporter of the period, Lincoln Steffens, said that violence and illegal activities stemmed from Prohibition, and Prohibition helped make crime pay. These were gangland killings, not routine Saturday night bar shootings or domestic squabbles with tragic endings. When mobsters killed, the police said, it was usually because of business, not passion. While moralists mounted massive anti-booze campaigns, gangsters mobilized networks of manufacturers, suppliers, and distributors to sell their wares throughout the country.

The Marlow rubout was just one example of the hundreds carried out around the country.

Prohibition was shrouded in a cloak of respectability by ministers, who delivered damning sermons on the evils of drinking, and there was a widespread movement of tattlers who would inform authorities whenever they encountered law-breakers.

Bolstered by criminal laws against the sale and use of alcoholic beverages, crime-busting federal agents made a name for themselves trying to destroy distilleries and warehouses where whiskey and beer were either made or stored for shipment to "speakeasies" all over America.

Mobsters viewed the laws prohibiting drinking as an unprecedented opportunity to make millions. The leaders of various crime families deftly mobilized massive manufacturing, shipping, and distribution networks to fill the sudden need for booze. By 1929, mobsters had widespread liquor operations throughout the country. Frank Marlow's death was a byproduct of this commerce.

The country was divided into designated franchises by the various crime families, who guarded their territories jealously. Murders became as commonplace as the speakeasies which sold "hooch" and foul-tasting gin. When one gang shot it out with another, it was more than just a clash of personalities. When machine guns were drawn to take down members of a rival gang, it was usually about business.

THE case of the Hotsy Totsy Club murders in New York is another prime example of mob violence that permeated the city's nightlife.

It was a hot night in July of 1929. In the Hotsy

Totsy Club the mood was mellow. Suddenly the door slammed open, and in burst a group of waterfront thugs, led by William and Peter Cassidy. The raucous crew swarmed over to the bar and demanded service. The bartender, busy serving other customers, ignored them.

"Hey, shithead," one of the Cassidy boys shouted, "you're not deaf. We came in here for a drink."

Instead of jumping, the bartender calmly continued to serve other customers. Others in the bar backed him up, shouting curses at the newcomers. Words were hurled back and forth, and when the brawlers made threatening moves toward other customers, they found themselves outmatched by gunmen, who suddenly cut loose.

When it was over, ex-con Simon Walker was dead, and longshoreman William "Red" Cassidy was mortally wounded.

Just another barroom brawl? Perhaps. But speculation ran high that the shooting had been staged by gunmen out to get the Cassidys in revenge for the Marlow killing. The shooting spree was nothing less than another gangland stunt to thwart an investigation aimed at identifying the killers.

In an attempt to build a case, the cops rounded up twenty-five people known to have been in the club that morning and brought them before a grand jury. The prosecutor portrayed the now dead William Cassidy as a longshoreman who actually made his money as a beer runner. In secret proceedings, two gunmen were named and a manhunt was launched to apprehend them.

When the indictments were made public, John "Legs" Diamond and an ex-con named Charles Entratta, sometimes known as Charlie Green, were named. Entratta had done a lot of time upstate for various crimes and was out on the street again, presumably working the same old rackets. Cassidy had worked as a strong-arm man for various known criminals. Simon Walker did a stretch in Sing Sing upstate and was armed with two guns when he got it. Jack Diamond, known as "Legs," always carried heat. He had been a bodyguard for Jacob Orgen, the late East Side mobster who had been recently gunned down in a shoot-out in which Diamond himself almost lost his life.

Both Entratta and Diamond had been brought up on murder charges numerous times.

"This time," a prosecutor said, "we've got a chance to prove it. We've got witnesses."

"I regard these as two very important indictments against two very notorious gunmen and racketeers," the police commissioner at the time declared, talking freely to reporters outside his office. "They will serve as a message to gangdom that the police will give them no quarter. This indictment brings to the fore the fact that gangdom is in control of the night clubs. It would be well for decent people to keep away from such places," the commissioner said, "for they're going to get a lot of police attention from now on."

A determined search for Diamond and Entratta ensued. Diamond was part-owner in the Hotsy Totsy Club. Police were also looking for Diamond's partner, Hymie Cohen, who was alleged to have ordered the band to keep playing during the shootout. According to witnesses, Diamond himself pumped a bullet into one of the Cassidys. When the man fell, Diamond is alleged to have stood over his body and emptied his gun into him. Police were now boasting that they had witnesses willing to testify. It made their case sound airtight.

Entratta was extradited from Chicago back to New York to face the charges. Diamond was detained. Soon bad things began to happen to witnesses. Waiter Thomas Merola was being held as a material witness. His lawyer tried to get him released, claiming that doctors said he suffered from psychosis, an ailment that would be aggravated if he remained jailed!

Hymie Cohen, Diamond's partner, turned up dead. Two waiters mysteriously died and the state's case against Diamond and Entratta began to deteriorate rapidly. Informants (police officers masquerading as gangsters) learned that all three had been taken out of state and killed.

"I have information that three of our Hotsy Totsy witnesses have been murdered," the commissioner said. "This information, gathered by members of the secret service squad, comes to us from sources we consider very reliable," he added. "Our information is that the people who committed the two murders in the Hotsy Totsy Club feared that Cohen would be a weak witness. They feared he might spill the beans. They had him murdered and the two others killed to make certain of their silence."

In March 1930, Diamond and Entratta were freed after the state's case against them collapsed. Too many witnesses had died and those who remained apparently got the message. Nobody saw anything—at least nothing they cared to share with the police.

In 1929, crime did pay. Marlow's killer went free. Legs Diamond went on to become one of New York's most notorious mobsters. In fact, a Broadway play called *Legs* was produced decades later, extolling the era of one of its most famous entrepreneurs.

Chapter 2
Legs Diamond

WHEN Jack "Legs" Diamond was shot in the fall of 1930, he steadfastly refused to finger his would-be assassins. It was a typical gangster response. Men like Legs were sworn to silence when it came to the cops. Besides, these mugs squeezed off a couple of shots but didn't do the job. Dubbed the "human ammunition dump" by newspaper writers of the era, there would be a total of five attempts to get Diamond, before someone ended the life and career of one of America's most notorious gangsters.

On Broadway, where his legend grew as his exploits were passed along the street by hustlers, con men, and other common elements, Legs Diamond was the romantic king of underworld figures. Upstate, in the Catskill Mountains, he was known as the country gentleman of South Durham. There, he built a fortress guarded by floodlights, and was known as the champion of the underprivileged, building porches for widows and passing out five-dollar tips to local merchants.

Diamond emerged from the streets of the Lower East Side, a training camp for many of the city's most powerful gang leaders. He got busted at seventeen for a minor burglary, did time in reform school, and wound up in trouble again after he took a hike without permission while serving in the U.S. Army. Other than that, however, he spent little time behind bars. Until four years before his death, Diamond played only bit parts in underworld sagas played out in the streets and back rooms of speakeasies all over the city. But in 1927, Jacob Orgen, known in the street as "Little Augie," was attacked by three men with guns.

Diamond's brother, Eddie, ordinarily served as Little Augie's bodyguard. But Legs was filling in for Eddie the day Little Augie got it. For his trouble, Legs took three bullets under the heart in a gunfight at the corner of Delancy and Norfolk Streets. It wouldn't be the last time. In fact, it was the state of a rather dubious legend—that it would take more than an ordinary bullet to knock off Diamond.

After the shoot-out, Legs was treated at Bellevue Hospital, where he was grilled by detectives. This, too, began another legend attached to Diamond: that he would never rat on anyone, even thugs who were trying to kill him. For his troubles, the cops tried to hang Little Augie's murder on him, saying he had led his boss into an ambush. Nevertheless, he was released and the charges were subsequently dropped. Even this minor incident led to still another Legs Diamond legend—he could be arrested repeatedly and never be convicted.

An example came with the death of mob boss Frank Marlow, a well-known mob figure on Broadway. Marlow, who was heavily involved in the manufacture, distribution, and sale of illegal alcoholic beverages at the height of Prohibition, was last seen near the Hotel Harding on West Fifty-Fourth Street. It was 1929, the same year the famous St. Valentine's Day Massacre occurred in Chicago. The Broadway Limited, an overnight train between New York and Chicago, was often used to transport mobsters from one jurisidiction to another. Legs Diamond was right in the thick of many illegal activities.

In June 1929, when the police found Frank Marlow dying outside a cemetery in Flushing, Queens, it was obvious that this had been a professional hit. Nine months later, Diamond was arrested in connection with Marlow's killing. He admitted he had taken a room at the Harding Hotel, near where Marlow was last seen alive, but Diamond denied any knowledge of the shooting.

"Marlow was just a beer-loader," Diamond was quoted as saying, "I wouldn't bother with a mug like that." The charges against him in the Marlow shooting were dismissed for lack of evidence.

A short time after Marlow, the cops came calling again—this time in connection with the Hotsy Totsy Club murders. William "Red" Cassidy and an ex-con named Simon Walker had been gunned down in the club. Diamond was the number one suspect, along with one Charles Entratta. Entratta was arrested and held without bail. Diamond disappeared. Eight months later, he strolled into police headquarters alone and surrendered to detectives. Entratta had already beat the rap because the state failed to prove its case. Since there was no case, there were no charges pending against Diamond.

In another incident, the cops began looking for Diamond in connection with a Brooklyn murder. Diamond again became a key suspect, but surrendering was the last thing on his mind this time. Beer-runner Harry Western was dead, and the cops wanted Diamond for questioning. Legs was busy arranging for whiskey shipments from Germany. He set sail for Europe, but when he tried to land on European shores, authorities forbade him to enter.

The *New York Times* ran an editorial, humorously chiding European governments for refusing to accept one of America's "most eminent" citizens. "Why are certain foreign countries so inhospitable?" the *Times* asked. "Mr. Legs Diamond is one of our most active businessmen and sportsmen. His skill with a racket is unexcelled. No crime survey is complete without him." The story went on to say that Scotland Yard chased him, and warned the Irish to keep him on the move. He was not even welcome in Belgium. Though his passport was in order, he was detained.

Diamond returned to the United States and arrived in Philadelphia, where he was arrested on the odd charge of being a "suspicious character." He agreed to leave the city and was released.

On the second Saturday in October 1930, Diamond arrived in Manhattan from his Catskills retreat, and was dropped off by two men at Grand Central Station. He walked the short distance to the Hotel Monticello on Sixty-Fourth Street, where he registered under an assumed name. He took the keys to Room 829, reserved for him by the manager, Jacob Ginsberg. The next morning, the gangster read the morning papers and lounged around, dressed in a pair of red silk pajamas. At 11:30, the door opened and three men walked in.

"Well, here we are," one of them said. "Let's go." They each produced weapons and began shooting.

"It knocked me over on the bed and they ran out," Diamond later recalled. "After a while, I got to my feet and went along the hall as far as the elevator. Then I fell over again and I don't remember anything until I came to in Ginsberg's room," he said

Rushed to the hospital by a private ambulance, Diamond wasn't expected to live. "Gangster, said to be dying, insists he does not know three who attacked him," the Monday morning headlines read. "Police patrol hospital."

Hospital security was beefed up after informants told the cops another attempt would be made on Diamond's life if he did not die shortly. "If Diamond didn't die before midnight," the informant said, "gunmen would swoop down on the hospital, battle their way into the room where he lay between life and death, and end his suffering with a broadside from their automatics."

THREE days later, Diamond was sitting up in bed at Polyclinic Hospital, sipping milk and holding court. Meanwhile, police rounded up known criminals, including rival Arthur Flegenheimer—Dutch Schultz—for questioning. Charlie Entratta, sometimes known as Charlie Green, was another bad boy brought in from his New Rochelle home for questioning. Schultz was heavily into booze shipments and a variety of rackets operating throughout the city. Entratta had been indicted along with Diamond for the 1929 Hotsy Totsy Club murders.

Schultz was implicated in Diamond's shooting because of a theory that the two had had a dispute over the death of a Schultz associate. Schultz allegedly threatened to kill Diamond in retaliation for the killing of Joe Noe, a long-time Schultz partner, the year before. It was believed that Diamond had had Noe killed in front of the Hotel Harding on West Fifty-Fourth Street near Broadway. Schultz however, disputed the theory.

A third man, Salvatore Arcidiaco, sometimes called Dannie Brocco, was also questioned. He said that he and Diamond had concocted a plan to travel to Europe together to buy cheap rye whiskey in Germany. The two had planned to meet in Germany, but German authorities detained Diamond and refused to allow him in the country, Arcidiaco told the cops. Schultz, Arcidiaco, and Entratta were cleared and later released.

Despite the story Diamond told them, police believed the shooting really stemmed from a dispute Diamond had with the three men shortly before the shooting. The three had met with Diamond to discuss racketeering profits and dispute ensued. The shooting started and Diamond got hit.

Whatever the reasons, the shooting was a near miss. Diamond had cheated assassins many times, surviving at least eleven bullets that somehow missed their mark over the years. "John Thomas Diamond was distinguished not only for his capacity for absorbing bullets, but for the ease with which he wriggled free of criminal charges. He was almost as good at one as the other—almost, but not quite," the *New York Times* wrote in the December 19, 1931 issue.

Legs Diamond was finally killed in an Albany rooming house in the early morning hours of December 18 as he slept in a drunken stupor after an exhausting night with his long-time girlfriend. The couple had been celebrating Diamond's most recent acquittal in a Troy, New

York, courtroom where he had beaten kidnapping charges.

"Three soft-nosed .38-caliber bullets fired from a pistol held against the back of his head did the job," read one newspaper account. "The gunmen left him lying on the bed with his arms at his side, his white face twisted in a dying leer. The position of the body indicated that one man held him while another did the shooting."

Witnesses later told police they had seen two men run from the building after shots were heard in the neighborhood. They got into a waiting maroon car and it sped away, heading north. A short time later, a police officer in the town of Saugerties spotted the car and took down the license plate number. Swarms of police descended on the Dove Street rooming house. Investigators from District Attorney John Delaney's office began to interview witnesses. By late afternoon, the authorities had pieced together the following story.

Diamond had rented three rooms on the second floor of the Dove Street rooming house about ten days earlier. He was accompanied by his wife, his sister-in-law, Mrs. Edward Diamond, and her ten-year-old son, John. He told the landlady his name was Kelly, just Mr. Kelly. However, the landlady, Laura Wood, learned his real identity two days later when she saw his picture next to a newspaper account of the Troy trial.

"When I found out, there was nothing I could do about it," Laura Wood told DA investigators. "They were quiet, in fact, he was quite the gentleman. People seemed to like him."

The jury only deliberated for five hours before returning the not guilty verdict. Diamond had been acquitted of kidnapping James Duncan. The Diamonds retired to a restaurant on Broadway in Albany where they celebrated until one o'clock in the morning. Legs got restless and announced he was leaving. His wife stayed on with the other partygoers.

"I've gotta go see some of my newspaper pals," he said. "I'll be gone about half an hour. Stick around till I get back," he told everyone, then left with his bodyguard.

Diamond, accompanied by chauffeur Jack Storey, instead went to see his girlfriend, Marion Roberts, who was staying nearby. "Gotta see Marion," Diamond said, in good spirits over his acquittal. Miss Roberts, a one-time New York chorus girl, was in town for Diamond's trial. While Storey waited outside, Diamond went in. He stayed upstairs until four in the morning, then staggered downstairs and ordered Storey to take him home. Forty-five minutes later, they arrived at the rooming house. Diamond slowly made his way upstairs to his room and the place was quiet again.

A short time later, according to residents, the early morning quiet was shattered by the sound of several gunshots. Residents told investigators they heard four or five shots, then the sound of running feet. Men crashed through the front door and ran across the street to the waiting vehicle. The landlady, Laura Wood, had been given the number of the Broadway restaurant in case of an emergency. She dialed the number and Mrs. Diamond answered.

"I think there's been a shooting," Mrs. Wood said. "You'd better hurry over." Mrs. Diamond arrived, followed by Diamond's personal physician, Dr. Thomas Holmes. Residents stood in the hallway, talking among themselves.

When she found Legs' body, Mrs. Diamond became hysterical. "Help me, somebody," she moaned. "They've shot Jack. Oh, they've killed him."

He had two bullets in his head. A third passed through his skull and was stuck in the bedpost.

Police arrived and began a fruitless search for suspects. A mile away, near St. Paul's Church, police found a pearl-handled pistol. Like most mob hits, theories over who killed Legs Diamond and why have flourished over the years. Storey had heard that a couple of Brooklyn thugs were in Albany, intent on doing him in. "What the hell do I care," Diamond responded.

Authorities said that Diamond had overstepped his bounds in his attempts to take over certain beer businesses. Another theory was that an unidentified New York gambler had hired someone to kill Diamond after he refused to pay a $25,000 gambling debt. Others said that a group of racketeers waited to see if Diamond would beat his kidnapping charges. If convicted, he would have been safely tucked away in prison. With his acquittal, they moved to eliminate him as a competitor.

Diamond had recently merged his forces with a Bronx thug named Vincent Coll, later to earn the sobriquet, "Mad Dog." Together, they had been waging a bitter war against Dutch Schultz for control of the Bronx. It was the Schultz connection that made the most sense to investigators.

Back in New York City, Diamond's death didn't come as a surprise.

"So they got him at last," one high-ranking police officer was quoted as saying. "He's no loss to the community, not to his community anyway. I am not surprised. I expected to see him taken long before this.''

"That man was responsible for many deaths around this city," another said.

"That's the way it is with all of them," the other officer said.

Chapter 3
Dutch Treat: Dutch Schultz

IT was just a theory, like most of the theories linked to a mob killing. Albert Stein, sometimes known as Al Stern, was a two-bit dope user who sometimes free-lanced as a shooter for the mob. In the fall of 1935 he got an assignment: get Dutch Schultz and Louis "Pretty" Amberg. Stein's rap sheet was proof enough that he was capable of crime. He had been fingered in at least seven underworld killings in the past few years and he was suspected of killing a cop. For these crimes he had earned the nickname "Mad Dog."

Stein's target, Dutch Schultz, *né* Arthur Flegenheimer, controlled one of the so-called "Jewish mobs" in New York, rivaling the "Italian families" for control of various city rackets. Some cops theorized that Stein, a twen-ty-two-year-old one-time member of Schultz's gang, was tapped by the Italian underworld to put Schultz away.

The killing was a gangland classic. Dutch was shot on October 23, 1935 as he and his associates pored over account books in a small dining room at the Palace

Chop House and Tavern on Park Street in Newark. At about 10:30 that night, two men armed with a machine gun and a sawed-off shotgun burst into the restaurant and opened fire. Schultz and three men with him were mortally wounded.

A short time later, Marty Krompier, a thirty-three-year-old lieutenant of Schultz's from Manhattan, and Samuel Gold of the Bronx, were attacked by four men in a barbershop on Broadway and shot repeatedly.

ACCORDING to newspaper stories, Schultz was "just an unambitious, sloppy, flat burglar and package thief in the Bronx." By the mid-1930s, however, he was among the most successful bootleggers around, with a fleet of delivery trucks rolling up the West Side to the 149th Street bridge with loads from the Phoenix Brewery. Schultz also laid claim to several lucrative numbers rackets. He controlled waiters' unions and managed a restaurant and nightclub.

With all of this going for him, he still looked like a vagrant, and was once described as "a perfect example of the unsuccessful man." It was a label Schultz seemed proud of, and he refused to wear well-tailored clothes. He liked to brag that he never paid more than fifty dollars for a suit of clothes, even if they fit worse than the hat on a junkman's horse. Once, during the trial of a friend in upstate New York, he chided associates for paying twenty bucks for silk shirts. "I never bought one in my life, and only a sucker will pay fifteen or twenty dollars for a silk shirt," the *New York Times* quoted him as saying.

DUTCH was born in the Bronx in 1902. His father was a saloon keeper, his mother a hardworking laundress who supported the family after his father deserted them. Dutch dropped out of school in the sixth grade, something he later regretted. He was a newsboy when he wasn't hanging out with members of the 149th Street gang in the South Bronx. An apprentice and card-carrying member of the roofers' union, Schultz did various odd jobs for brief stints.

His true career began in the winter of 1919, when he was busted for burglarizing an apartment. He was sentenced to an indeterminate term on Blackwell's Island. Not a model prisoner, he was transferred to Westhampton Farms. He escaped once, and wound up spending a total of fifteen months in jail. When Arthur Flegenheimer returned to the Bronx, his reputation earned him the nickname ''Dutch'' Schultz, despite the fact that he came from German-Jewish stock. The name was borrowed from a boxer well-known among the old Frog Hollow gang, and fit his tough personality.

After 1919, Dutch never spent another minute behind bars, despite thirteen arrests, including several for murder and assault. Schultz's key to success was his ability to organize. Working as a strong-arm on beer trucks, Schultz branched out for himself in 1928. He teamed up with Joe Noe to run a speakeasy on Brook Avenue. They bought three old trucks, hired drivers and strong-arm men, and made nightly beer runs from New Jersey to the Bronx, buying their brew from Frankie Dunn who owned a brewery in Union City.

At one point, Schultz acquired a warehouse in the Bronx, then bought a larger one on Third Avenue. Using ferries to bring illegal goods into New York was too slow, so Schultz teamed up with Frenchy Dillon and Jay Culhane. They owned breweries in Paterson and Yonkers. Schultz now bought his beer from Yonkers.

Up to this point, it had been luck and luck alone that kept Schultz in business. But in 1929, he got smart and used some of his profits to buy protection. His empire grew, according to police records, and by 1931 he owned seventeen beer drops in the metropolitan area, where he stored large quantities of the illegal drink, supplying a wide network of buyers. Many of his operations were sophisticated places, including one known as "The Tins." It was alleged to have a disappearing elevator which took empty beer trucks underground. When they reappeared, they were fully loaded. He no longer had to import brew from out-of-town locations. It was a good arrangement for everybody, Schultz and the midtown beer barons.

With them as his protective partners, Schultz took over distribution on the Upper West Side and Harlem to the north, and he moved as far south as Fourteenth Street downtown. Ambitions to spread out even further put him in direct conflict with Bugsy Siegel and the guns of Waxy Gordon, who dominated the West Side action. Schultz wasn't blind, and he knew the score. His first partner, Joe Noe, had been iced in a shootout on Fifty-Fourth Street. When he began spreading out, Schultz knew that Bugsy Siegel and Waxy Gordon were capable of more than bad-mouthing him on the street.

But in 1931, Schultz confronted internal problems when two of his boys decided to hack off a piece of the Harlem action for themselves. Vinnie "Mad Dog" Coll, a cold-blooded boxer who worked for Schultz and Charles "Fats McCarthy" Papke, staged a series of raids on Schultz's College Avenue garage and knocked off several beer caravans. Drivers were killed and payrolls were snatched. Some of Schultz's people were roused in the middle of the night. The boys were taking hundreds of thousands of dollars in cash, and destroyed thousands more in slot machines, trucks, and other vital equipment. Fearing for his life, The Dutchman went underground. Even the strong midtown bosses didn't want to tangle with the crazies who were now running with "Mad Dog" Coll. The feud ended in a blaze of machine-gun fire weeks later when Vinnie took an "urgent telephone call" at the corner drugstore near the Cornish Arms Hotel on Twenty-Third Street, where he had been living. Once Coll was disconnected, Schultz came out of hiding to continue spiraling upward in the Manhattan rackets.

He ousted Caspar Holstein, a numbers man who controlled the rackets in Harlem, after Holstein failed to pay Schultz on a $10,000 loan. Schultz also took over other policy operations, got control of the waiters' union, and money began to pour in from a variety of directions. He spent undisclosed amounts of it on political protection.

Politically, he could fix just about any legal beef in New York, Connecticut, or the reaches of Pennsylvania. However, the Feds pinned an income tax evasion rap on him, something his local connections would have little influence over.

How could a punk like Al Stern get to Schultz when the smartest lawmen in the Northeast couldn't nail him, and the toughest gangsters couldn't take him out? Clues linking Stern to Schultz's murder were tentative at best: that he lived in a rooming house in the center of Newark's Italian lottery rackets, chief rivals of Schultz, and he had been known as a hired killer who had once worked for Schultz.

But as Deputy Chief Haller maintained throughout the investigation, Stern was just a small-time drug addict, not a trained assassin. To make his point, he showed reporters the small, .32-caliber pistol Stern had used in a routine stick-up shortly before his death. "I ask you," Haller said, holding up the pistol, "is that a gunman? It is my belief that Schultz was shot by one of his own mob, not purposely, but accidentally," Haller said. Schultz's body had .45-cliber slugs in it. "We believe the .45s belonged to Schultz's men. Schultz, of the four men shot, was the only one shot by a .45-caliber slug; all the rest had .38-caliber or shotgun slugs," he told the *New York Times*.

Among the wounded taken to Newark City Hospital were Schultz and Bernard Rosenkrantz, who doubled as bodyguard and chauffeur for Schultz. Also in the hospital were Otto Biederman, sometimes called Otto Berman, and a third man, Abraham Landau, sometimes called Leo Frank. Rosenkrantz had been shot at least twelve times and died the day after the shooting. Police, who maintained a bedside vigil, questioned Rosenkrantz, Biederman, and Landau but none of the wounded men could speak coherently. Biederman, although only shot once, suffered a severed artery, and he, too, died shortly after Rosenkrantz and Landau.

Martin Krompier, Schultz's chief lieutenant, was taken to Polytechnic Hospital in New York. He and bookmaker Samuel Gold were hit in a midtown barbershop almost two hours after Schultz got it across the river in New York.

Schultz, aware that he was mortally wounded, called for a priest and was given Last Rites in the hospital—an unusual request for a Jew to make.

Doctors gave him repeated blood transfusions, hoping to revive him. People went underground, hiding out in Staten Island, Queens, and in the northern Bronx.

Schultz's statements, recorded word for word, revealed a number of well-known crime figures. Schultz either refused to identify his killers or simply could not because of his condition. When asked who had shot him, he said "The Boss," a nickname used by notorious gangster Charles "Lucky" Luciano, a high-ranking mobster. The hits certainly had the earmarks of a major Mafia operation.

Schultz repeatedly slipped into delirium, mumbling things which were largely unintelligible. One of the names he mentioned repeatedly in connection with large sums of money was the name "John." Authorities theorized that he was referring to Johnny Torrio, a major Chicago crime figure who rose to power after the celebrated hit of "Big" Jim Colissimo. Torrio's name had recently become well-known in New York political circles, and had been linked to Manhattan First Assembly District leader Albert Marinelli by one of his political opponents. It was possible, police speculated, that the wealthy Torrio could have moved in on Schultz and thus become the new boss.

Schultz's ramblings were earmarked by his colorful way of phrasing things, including a wide array of nicknames and street slang. He said things like "get the doll a roofing," street talk for "find a girl a place to live." He called out for his mother and referred to himself as "Hitler," a nickname given to him by Bo Weinberg and Marty Krompier. He used the name "Chinaman" several times during his rantings, a reference to a guy named Chink Sherman, a rival with whom Schultz had had some difficulties years earlier.

But the most important clue that came from Schultz's death-bed rantings was the name "Boss."

A citywide dragnet went up and detectives and beat cops were ordered to pick up Charles "Lucky" Luciano in connection with the shooting. Luciano was the reputed head of the *Unione Siciliano* in New York, a secret organization with arms that stretched across the U.S. Luciano was its most recent "boss" in New York City.

Frank Yale, alleged to have been killed by Capone's men in Brooklyn, once headed the *Unione* in New York. Luciano subsequently became its leader. He was picked up and taken downtown for questioning. He had earned the name "Lucky" in gangland circles because it was said that he was the only known gangster who had returned alive after being "taken for a ride" by rivals. In that incident, he was shot and left in Staten Island for dead. He recovered from his wounds and lived to become the most powerful underworld boss on the East Coast.

Luciano took over despite savage attempts by rivals to rub him out. Police said he won the top spot in the *Unione Siciliano* after killing Giuseppe Masseria, known as "Joe The Boss," a leading crime figure in the Coney Island section of Brooklyn who was killed in 1931.

Schultz had lost his grip on the rackets he controlled in the city while he fought off federal income tax charges the year before his murder. While he was trapped in court battles, rival gangs systematically took control of his operations, knocking out Schultz associates in large numbers. Although ultimately acquitted of the tax charges in Albany, Schultz found himself exiled to towns and cities just outside New York. In fact,

Mayor Fiorello La Guardia warned Schultz that he would be arrested on the spot if he set foot in the city.

Bo Weinberg became a Schultz emissary, commissioned with the risky job of warning rival gang members that he intended to retain control of a wide range of rackets. According to police files, this prompted Schultz rivals in Manhattan, Brooklyn, and Newark to send back an equally serious message to back off or face the consequences. Weinberg disappeared a short time later. It had been rumored that he had been shot and his body, shoved into a barrel filled with cement, had been dumped into the Hudson.

The only gang to stand by The Dutchman was a bunch headed by Louis "Pretty" Amberg, a Brooklyn racketeer. While Schultz had set up temporary headquarters at the Robert Treat Hotel in Newark, Amberg was sequestered in a midtown Manhattan hotel. Just days before Schultz was clipped, Amberg's body was found in a burning car near the Brooklyn Navy Yard.

While cops collected various theories for Schultz's demise, speculation that a small-time hood like Stein, whose body was found in the shabby room he occupied, had been the actual hit man, faded into the background. Police said that a racial or ethnic war was at least part of the motive behind Schultz's death. However, that idea eventually took a backseat to a more plausible theory.

Special Prosecutor Thomas Dewey, who had launched a widespread investigation into racketeering, said that rival gangs had pushed into every corner of the Schultz empire. They had been successful in operating loan-sharking, gambling, and union activities and selling illegal booze. Their takeover had been done quietly and efficiently.

Highly placed police and political officials had been paid off, and the newcomers had been able to operate without interference. Dewey said with the threat of Schultz reclaiming his turf, widespread publicity was sure to follow. Schultz was a highly visible figure, and the new gangs wanted to keep things quiet: another Luciano trademark. Even if Schultz had been satisfied with a piece of their action, (which he had already refused), the publicity surrounding his return to the city would attract too much heat.

In his hospital room, Schultz received odd messages, apparently from friends and enemies alike. One said "Keep the white elephant busy," a reference to a good luck charm he'd gotten from a woman friend in Syracuse, New York. From Harlem he got a telegram which said "Don't be yellow. As ye sow, so shall ye reap." It was signed "Madame Sinclair, Policy Queen," according to a story in the *New York Times*.

Doctors and nurses who attended Schultz, said that he knew he was dying and called out for his mother repeatedly. Shortly before he slipped into a final coma, he told them, "This is the journey's end. It's death for me." Then he fell unconscious and died.

Police informants said the vacuum left by the sudden demise of two criminal kingpins—Schultz and Amberg—was filled quickly. A consortium of gangland leaders assumed control of the various rackets once controlled by the two powerful leaders. Although police said they knew who the new kingpins were, they were unable to find evidence linking them to either hit.

One of the new leaders was Johnny Torrio, who allegedly lost his clout in the Midwest to Al Capone. Aligned with Torrio were Charlie "Lucky" Luciano, Meyer Lansky, Louis "Lepke" Buchalter, Charles

"Buck" Siegel, Jacob "Gurrah" Shapiro, and Abe "Longy" Zwillman.

When Schultz was killed, police speculated that his murder involved a turf war with one of the New York gang factions. When questioned about his killers, Schultz died silently, never revealing what he must have known: that he was a victim of Murder, Inc., not the greed of a rival.

FIVE years after Schultz was killed, "Kid Twist" Reles was picked up in connection with the brutal slaughter of Whitey Rudnick. Rudnick had been strangled, and he'd been stabbed at least sixty times. His skull had also been fractured. "Whitey got it because he was a stool pigeon," Reles told Brooklyn District Attorney William O'Dwyer.

His words were both ironic and prophetic. For more than a year, the Kid fingered his associates, implicating them in some 200 murders. In total, he said the national syndicate had committed between 400 and 500 murders in the decade beginning in 1930.

Pittsburgh Phil was nailed for at least one hundred of these alone. Bugsy Goldstein was convicted for the killing of gambler Puggy Feinstein. Both men eventually went to the electric chair. Mendy Weiss, Louis Capone (no relation to Alphonse), Frank "The Dasher" Abbandando, and Happy Maione were also executed. The highest ranking member, Louis Lepke, was himself convicted of murder and executed. The only remaining kingpin was Albert Anastasia, the Lord High Executioner. Squad member Charlie Workman, charged with the Schultz killing, saw the handwriting on the wall. He pleaded guilty and was sentenced to life imprisonment.

Chapter 4
Gennacide

THE legendary Genna family once reigned supreme in Chicago's Little Italy. We will taste a potpourri of violence featuring regular murder for profit, revenge, and in one case for sheer maliciousness. We'll see "Bloody" Angelo Genna, full of spaghetti and wine, rise from his post-pradial semi-torpor and gun down a man he didn't care for much; and later we'll mark his own sudden passing. Called the "scabarous clan" by one crime writer, the Gennas were special and brought an almost magical mindlessness to crime that could only have flourished in Chicago in the Roaring Twenties.

Few Sicilian crime families fought Americanization more than the Gennas. They did their best to keep the Old World ways of violence and extortion intact and probably would have been happier as good old-fashioned "Black Handers," working with "Lupo the Wolf," an old-time Mafioso, a decade or two earlier.

The Gennas operated stills during the reign of Big

Al Capone. They hailed from the village of Marsala, Sicily, where women wore black and men filled graves. They were not lovable but they were feared.

By applying native guile, treachery, and ferocity, they soon found themselves virtual masters of Little Italy during Prohibition. They had many strong-arms to help them, none stronger than the fearsome likes of fellow Marsala townsmen, John Scalise and Alberto Anselmi. This pair was credited with inventing the Sicilian handshake where one of the pair would clasp a fellow player by the hand and say, for example: "How are you, Meester Frank, my good fren'?" while the straight man shot him in the back.

They are also credited with the practice of rubbing garlic on their bullets in the hope of nasty aftereffects.

Also serving the Genna family with distinction were the likes of Orazio "The Scourge" Tropea, who was believed by many in his neighborhood to have the power of the *malocchio,* the evil eye.

The Gennas controlled the sale of liquor in their territory; unfortunately, no one controlled the Gennas when they distilled it. It was almost better to be shot at than to drink the stuff—all who imbibed (and countless did) became ill, sooner or later. A few went blind or actually died. The clan knew how to contribute to a community.

The Genna empire prospered in relative peace for a time, as their poisonous stills hummed busily and money flowed in. During those calm days, the Irish shadow of Mr. Dion O'Banion fell over some of their territory. There's nobody, they used to say, nicer than a nice Irishman, or meaner than a mean one. O'Banion was a little of both. He loved flowers and ran a successful florist shop, catering to major gangland funerals. He helped make the "Chicago funeral" an institution, like the Texas cookout. He was a bit racist (though he liked Jews) and mistook the Genna pigheadedness for a lack of cunning. He tried to muscle in here and there and soon got to shake hands with Anselmo and Scalise. They won the battle but also won the undying enmity of Frank Gusenberg, the unforgiving Hymie Weiss, and warlord George "Bugs" Moran. This was to prove a problem down the line.

Capone always supported the Gennas, even though he was Neapolitan, but when he made his bid to take control of the venerated and utterly exclusive *Unione Siciliano* the Gennas, like most Sicilians, were filled with fury. This was a mortal insult; after all, tradition is tradition.

"Bloody" Angelo Genna went as far as to proclaim himself head of the *Unione,* and commissioned his favorite team of tiptoeing killers, Anselmi and Scalise, to avenge their honor on Big Al himself. It was 1925, the height of Capone's power, and Capone was the Patton of street-fighting, even if his broad-range strategies were a shade narrow. With a Costello or Luciano as his *consigliere* he might have been able to tone down his style and blend his organization into the background and draw less publicity. But he was spoiled by the wild west aspects of Chicago, as, certainly, were the Gennas.

The wily A & S approached Capone, betrayed Genna, and became his secret men. So began the Gennas' fatal slide to oblivion.

One sunny afternoon in Little Italy, Genna and three "button men" (paid assassins) had just finished packing away a tremendous lunch of spaghetti and meatballs. Tomato sauce dotted Angelo's collar, we are told, and he is said to have burped with contentment as he came out on the sidewalk, picking his teeth.

His dull brown eyes fell upon a certain Paul Labriola, a minor city hall employee, heading back to work. Labriola was a campaign worker for a mayorial candidate whom Genna disliked intensely. Despite the wine and pasta churning peacefully within him, Genna conceived an inspired political move.

As Labriola nervously headed across the street, avoiding eye contact with Genna, Samuzzo "Samoots" Amatuna, Johnny "Two-Gun" Guardino, and Frank "Don Chick" Gambino (no relation), Angelo gave the word. Pedestrians dodged as the bright afternoon exploded with a volley of gunfire that shattered Labriola and left him twitching in the gutter.

Angelo sauntered over, still picking his teeth,

"He ain't done yet,' he observed.

Mr. "Samoots" Amatuna concurred. Angelo stood over the man and blew holes in his head, then squinted like a craftsman at his handiwork.

"He's done now." He nodded.

The four men strolled to their car and drove calmly away. This was at the height of Genna rule in Little Italy, and no one said a word or saw a thing.

In May 1925, Angelo was honeymooning at Chicago's Belmont Hotel. He went out alone one day with enough cash in his pockets to buy a house (the domestic mood full upon him) when he noticed Dion O'Banion's minions on his trail.

Angelo fled. Frank Gusenberg, Hymie Weiss, "Bugs" Moran, and Vinnie "The Schemer" Drucci followed in hot pursuit.

Wildly turning to escape, Angelo hit a pole and was pinned behind the wheel while his car smoked and hissed. The boys liked that. They drove very slowly past him, savoring the scene.

"Look at that stupid fuck," "Bugs" is supposed to have said gleefully as they cut loose with a sustained volley of shotgun blasts that chewed him into chopped meat, as he was unable to do more than curse and fume and thrash.

"Die, you son of a bitch!" screamed Hymie Weiss.

Later that day at the morgue, a distraught Mike "El Diablo" Genna stood beside the ravaged body of his brother and made the Sicilian sign, *Morti a tutti*, meaning "death to everybody!" He immediately called on his two master assassins, crying "Get them pieces of shit, then stinking Christ-beating bastards, them goat rectums! Them puddles of dog piss! Kill them! Kill them, you hear me?!" Anselmi and Scalise understood their mission perfectly.

But more black treachery lay ahead, and the shadowy hand of fate itself was about to twist the threads of the drama. Telling Mike "The Devil" they had a line on his enemies, they got him into a car to be in on the kill. While they were deciding where to give him the bad news (in the form of a bullet in the head), they were spotted by a squad car carrying four interested detectives. They gave chase. Ironically enough, Mike "The Devil" sped off but seemed to have no more Richard Petty in him than his brother had and promptly ran into a telegraph pole.

The three mobsters jumped out and knelt, their shotguns ready. The cop car pulled up, and the first cop got out and asked why they hadn't stopped. His answer was a barrage of bullets.

The next man, half out of the car, was blasted back inside, fatally hit as well. The third cop was killed a second later. The last cop was a young rookie named Sweeney.

The deadly trio waited to pick him off when he showed his head. Sweeney showed a lot more. He kicked through the door and charged the gangsters, two pistols blazing away.

This wasn't what Anselmi and Scalise expected and they fled, beating "The Devil" to the nearest alleyway. Genna got hit in the leg as he dove into a cellar. Two off-duty cops had joined Sweeney, and they burst into the basement to get Genna, who was trying to conceal himself behind a coal pile. They took away his weapon and dragged him back outside, where an ambulance was waiting. As they rolled him onto the stretcher he managed to kick an attendant in the teeth and knock him senseless, snarling: "Take that, you fucking son of a bitch!"

Genna had been shot in an artery, and he bled to death within two hours. However, there was speculation that they just didn't hurry at the emergency room. Anselmi and Scalise were caught but never stood trial, thanks to Capone's influence.

Tony "The Gent" Genna laid low, but was lured to his doom by another traitor, gunman Giuseppe Nerone, who convinced him to meet to discuss the future. There wasn't much left to talk about. As they stood in the doorway of a Genna grocery store, Nerone shook his boss' hand. That should have told him something. Almost at once two Sicilians, one tall and skinny and the other short and squat, showed up out of nowhere and pumped half a dozen shots into Tony's back.

Genna lingered a few days in the hospital, long enough to name his killer to his girlfriend. But well before the cops ever got to talk to Nerone, he was shot to shreds in his favorite barber chair. After this the Gennas and ex-Genna men fell like bowling pins. "The Scourge" Tropea fell; Vito Boscone knelt and begged for mercy with clasped hands. The assassins shot off his hands first. Anselmi and Scalise were sorry they missed that one, but they got their licks in with Ecola "The Eagle" Baldelli, who fought back so savagely they ended up chopping his body to pieces and tossing the parts on a garage heap.

"Go in the garbage, you cocka-suck," Anselmi muttered.

It was over. One Genna ran back to Marsala, Sicily, to hide and went to jail for stealing holy relics in a church, closing his career on a positive note.

Chapter 5
Baseball Bat Dessert:
Anselmi and Scalise

THE Roaring Twenties were nearly over when Giuseppe "Hop Toad" Giunta was installed in 1929 as the new president of the ill-starred *Unione Siciliano,* with Anselmi and Scalise as his joint vice presidents. One night in Chicago in a brothel, Scalise waxed expansive. He was having a snort with his partner and was feeling pretty good. They'd killed off rival mobsters galore, were being well-paid by Capone, and honored by their countrymen.

"We're gonna be the big shots now," the lanky killer said to one of his floozies, while his squat, balding partner nodded in agreement.

This, however, didn't escape the attention of Frankie Rio, who was seated nearby. He was one of Big Al's top bodyguards, and he took his job seriously. He sensed that the deadly duo, now that the smoke had temporarily cleared, might well be restless again. After all, they hadn't changed sides or betrayed anybody for awhile.

Rio decided to talk to his boss. Big Al wasn't the

most suspicious man who ever lived (there were, after all, Vlad the Impaler and Shaktai, King of the Zulus), but he was close. He had once tested his friends by going from house to house in the middle of the night with a paper bag. He said there was a head in it, and he needed help to get rid of it. The ones who didn't gag and shut the door passed his test.

This time Big Al would test A & S. He and Rio staged a public argument that got ugly. Capone cursed and then slapped his lieutenant under the judicious eyes of the new vice presidents. Later, true to form, Anselmi and Scalise approached Rio and told him that Joey Aiello, a former partner and head of the *Unione*, had a price of $50,000 on Capone's head. Why not share the reward and do all of Sicily a service at the same time, plus take power with them and "Hop Toad" Giunta? Rio said he'd consider it, because he hated that fat fucking Capone, and so on.

Three days later, everybody who was anybody in the Capone crew met for dinner at a big round table in a private room. Everybody was eating heartily. Capone made a big speech about friendship and honor and loyalty. Then, as Anselmi and Scalise watched in stunned silence, he reached behind him, grabbed a baseball bat, and proceeded to savagely beat them to death in front of the family.

Capone had again demonstrated his ruthless control with another trademark performance. It was a night and a lesson not soon to be forgotten.

In 1987, director Brian DePalma reprised that scene in his movie *The Untouchables*. When Robert De Niro, as Al Capone, bludgeoned his rivals with a cold-blooded passion, "Scarface" himself would have approved.

Chapter 6
The Long Leak:
Joe "The Boss" Masseria

IT wasn't news that the cops wanted to talk to Joseph Masseria, known both in crime and police circles as "Joe The Boss." Joe, born in Sicily as Giuseppe, was a kingpin in 1920s' gangland circles. Beginning as early as 1922, criminals ruled the streets of New York and Joe the Boss led the pack, wielding Old-World brutality, meting out eye-for-an-eye justice wherever necessary

A thug named Edward Winger was shot on Rivington Street, and when police tried to get him to say who his assailants were, Winger closed his eyes and died without uttering a word. Things had gotten out of hand. The mayor formed a crime commission in an attempt to quell the mob-related violence. Warring bootleggers were knocking each other off as if somebody were giving out prizes. Abductions and murders were commonplace, and the metropolitan area resembled Dodge City.

While New Yorkers believed they had strict gun control laws, criminals simply lied on their applications for permits—when they bothered to get them at all. Arms were easily available across the river in New Jersey and through mail order houses located all over the country. Masseria was packing a pistol when he was hauled in for questioning in connection with the death of Silvio Sagilocompe, a gangland thug, who was killed in a crossfire between two rival gangs one morning along East Fourth Street.

"If I find that Masseria had no right to carry a pistol in this city . . . I shall request the grand jury to indict Masseria on a felony charge for carrying the weapon," one zealous but naive district attorney announced before the crime commission. He may as well have announced that he was revoking Masseria's birthday.

Joe The Boss was also suspected of bumping off Frank Marlow in the summer of 1929. He made no bones about who his friends were, but he streadfastly denied knowing who bumped off Marlow. Eventually, the cops had to let him go after three hours of tough questioning. It would take more than a hot light and a couple of cops to get the likes of Masseria to talk.

Police officials told reporters who followed the story that they had gotten nothing of significance from Masseria, except for learning that he had been in jail before. In fact, he had a police record that had begun more than twenty-two years earlier. Now, at the age of forty-three, being questioned by the police was all in a day's work for The Boss.

So, who was this Joe "The Boss" Masseria? First, and most prominently, he was the undisputed boss of the New York Mafia in the 1920s. He achieved that rank the only way possible in those days—by killing off his rivals.

Masseria arrived in America from Sicily at the turn

of the century, already firmly entrenched in Mafia circles. He teamed up with Lupo the Wolf, said to be either an uncle or cousin. It was Lupo who apparently maintained the so-called Murder Stable in East Harlem, an ad hoc graveyard for deceased rivals. Between them Masseria and Lupo headed a feared extortion ring that terrorized Italian immigrants. When Lupo got busted for counterfeiting, Masseria took over.

When Prohibition came, Masseria controlled household wine-making operations, common among immigrants who fermented wine mostly for their own use. He accumulated immense profits from his bootlegging operations, making him the most powerful and feared man in New York at the time. Immediately, he adopted a Golden Rule in order to maintain his lofty position. Whenever any rival became too powerful or rich, Joe The Boss bumped him off.

A phrase that would later become common on the street, however, applied to life in mob circles in the 1920s as well—what goes around, comes around. It meant that while Joe was busy plotting the demise of the competition, they were making funeral arrangements, too—for Masseria.

Two killers jumped him as he emerged from his Second Avenue apartment in Manhattan. "Joe The Boss darted into a millinery shop, trailed by the gunners, whose bullets shattered windows and mirrors and hit Masseria's straw hat twice," according to one account of the incident. "But they missed the Italian gangster, who thereby gained the mystique of being able to dodge bullets." He wouldn't be the last to make such a claim of invincibility, including the likes of Lucky Luciano and Legs Diamond, gangsters still in their formative years when Masseria was boss in New York circles.

Following his close call with Valenti's boys, Masseria made it known that he wanted peace between them. He asked for a "sit-down." They met in a restaurant on East Twelfth Street, where Masseria "pledged his loyalty to his new 'brother.' "

As they left the restaurant, Masseria draped his arm over Valenti's shoulders. On the sidewalk, Joe The Boss suddenly moved away and Valenti was cut down by a hail of bullets. So much for Joe's loyalty oaths.

By all accounts, no outsider dared to challenge Masseria's power for years. Then came a serious challenge which Joe The Boss could not ignore. It came form Salvatore Maranzano, an ambitious man who made it known that he would some day be known as "The Boss of All Bosses." War between them broke out, and bodies from both sides littered the streets. Maranzano was out-gunned by at least two to one.

Masseria had gained the loyalty of some of the biggest names in crime. In fact, a list of his top supporters included Lucky Luciano, Willie Moretti, Albert Anastasia, Carlo Gambino, Joe Adonis, and Frank Costello. They were his greatest strength—and in the end, his greatest weakness.

Masseria finally felt safe. In addition to these top lieutenants, he had dozens of "savage killers" to fight this brutal war. Among his top aides, Masseria favored Anastasia, who shared his philosophy of solving problems by murder. However, everyone admitted that Luciano was his most cunning assistant, a brilliant schemer and organizer.

But Masseria's blind spot was a flaw many businessmen have—the inability to accept valuable advice from within their own organization.

Masseria's power relied on Sicilian methods and

manners. The new men kept telling the old *capos* to make deals with other groups, like the Irish and the Jews. Luciano and Adonis had already begun working with Bugsy Siegel and Meyer Lansky, leaders of the so-called Jewish mob.

Costello was among the first in the organization to systematically pay off politicians, something that got Masseria's back up even more. He believed in bribing an official now and then, but he didn't want to sleep with them. Ironically, Masseria feared that close association with politicians would corrupt his gang members.

Masseria's biggest flaw, however, was believing that he had won the undying loyalty of the ambitious men who surrounded him.

Joe The Boss failed to understand that these younger men were as contemptuous of him as they were of Maranzano. They called the old men "Mustache Petes," referring to the handlebar mustaches worn by turn-of-the-century immigrants. As far as the young lieutenants were concerned Masseria and his rival Maranzano stood in the way of progress. These young lords had already put a plan into motion to stop the war between the two gangs so they could get back to their main business—making money.

The wars waged by old Sicilian dinosaurs weren't good for business. A truce was called between the young lions on both sides, and for a while, the lieutenants were content to wait until one gang leader successfully hit the other.

However, things moved too slowly. By 1931, Masseria and Maranzano showed no sign of stepping down. It was decided that nature needed a little help.

On April 15, 1931, Luciano invited Masseria to Coney Island for lunch. They ate at a popular underworld place, Nuova Villa Tammaro. About 3:30 P.M., Luciano went to the men's room. Moments later, four men came through the door: Vito Genovese, Joe Adonis, Albert Anastasia, and Bugsy Siegel. They drew their guns simultaneously and fired at Masseria. Six bullets hit him. The reign of Joe The Boss had ended.

Luciano told police, "I was in the can taking a leak. I always take a long leak."

This was the first move in the Luciano-Lansky plan to set up a new national crime syndicate. It was an historic moment for organized crime.

Chapter 7
Gottvater: Meyer Lansky

WHILE Meyer Lansky made great headlines (especially in his later years, when the Feds pressed to lock this mob giant up) this legend among crime figures remained a mystery. Throughout his rise to power, Lansky was linked with murder and mayhem but he was never convicted of any violent crime. While he remained a shadowy figure, it was common knowledge among mob insiders that Lansky was a respected member of the famous Commission, which oversaw the day-to-day business of policing the activities of the nation's organized crime families. In this way, Lansky presided over decisions to murder various Mafioso found guilty of breaking the rules. While he wasn't considered the Godfather of a particular fiefdom like Little Italy in New York, he was, in a sense, the *capo* of the National Crime Syndicate beginning in the early 1930s.

Lansky inherited the power of the warring Prohibition gangs as well as of the original Mafia. In particular, he inherited the turf of Giuseppe "Joe The Boss"

Masseria and Salvatore Maranzano, who were both killed, leaving Luciano and Lansky alive to absorb their holdings. Lansky, a Jew from Grodno, Poland, and Luciano, a Sicilian, are credited with ending an era with the deaths of Masseria and Maranzano.

Lansky was no angel but he often leaned on the thug-like personality of his underling, Bugsy Siegel. Together they ran what became one of the most violent and vicious of the Prohibition gangs. With Lansky as leader, these two formed the feared Bugs and Meyer gang specializing in booze hijackings. They became known as the protectors of bootleggers and their services went to the highest bidder.

Bugs and Meyer provided "slammings" and rubouts for a fee, and were the forerunners of Murder, Inc. Indeed, Lansky helped form Murder, Inc., encouraging enforcers to work under Louis Lepke, Albert Anastasia, and Bugsy Siegel. Other leaders of the new national crime syndicate didn't approve of the bloodthirsty Siegel, feeling he was too close to Lansky. Bugsy was dropped from the murder combine, but Lansky's influence increased. It was said that no major assignment for Murder, Inc. was ever approved without consulting him, including the 1947 killing of his long-time partner in crime, Siegel himself.

Siegel got himself in trouble during his push to create a gambling paradise in Las Vegas. When more than one million dollars of the mob's money turned up missing, Siegel's name was submitted to the crime commission as a hit target. Lansky's part in the final decision to allow the hit varies, depending upon which version of the story you hear. One says Lansky was forced to allow the hit, saying he had no choice but to vote along with the other members of the crime commission.

Another version was that Lansky himself insisted that his former partner be iced, after he was given time to produce gambling profits for the mob in Vegas.

As early as the 1920s, Lansky's talent for aligning himself with the right men at the right time was apparent. Luciano and Lansky conceived of the syndicate in the 1920s. Luciano was in his early twenties and Lansky was only eighteen. Together they fought the gang wars of the 'twenties and 'thirties, using brains when they lacked firepower.

When Luciano/Lansky hit Masseria and clipped Maranzano, they were on top. Not even Al Capone dared fight them.

"I learned a long time before that Meyer Lansky understood the Italian brain almost better than I did," Luciano was quoted as saying. "That's why I picked him to be my *consigliere*. I used to tell Lansky that he may've had a Jewish mother, but someplace he must've been wet-nursed by a Sicilian." Lansky, he said, "could look around corners" and anticipate what the right moves were. Luciano said, "the barrel of his gun was curved," an expression that suggested that Lansky could get an opponent easily while keeping himself out of the line of fire.

Lansky's ability to make smart decisions, eliminate competition, and remain alive were traits that ensured him a long and illustrious career. He never resented Luciano's top position; he preferred safety and avoided almost all publicity. Just staying alive as he tried to establish himself as a power among cold, ambitious men was a feat in itself. "Gang warfare, sometimes dormant but never dead, flames anew with bitterness unequaled since repeal of Prohibition," the *New York Times* said. Internal warfare between rivals claimed the lives of at least a dozen gangsters between August and October of 1935. Another dozen wiseguys had been wounded in shoot-outs all over New York. Lansky was among the chief architects of this new, emerging pecking order.

One round of gang killings in the fall of 1935 ended in a thirty-six-hour blitz. First Louis Amberg was found in a burning car; a month earlier, his brother Joseph had been discovered dead in a downtown garage. The day after Amberg got it, two gunmen broke into a Newark tavern and blew Dutch Schultz away, taking three bodyguards with him. An hour later, a henchman of Schultz was killed in a Manhattan barbershop.

Did Schultz maneuver the Amberg deaths and was he shot in retaliation? Or was he shot by his own subordinates who resented his "undeserved" lofty position? Or did the Ambergs and Schultz have a common enemy?

The third possibility speaks volumes when one considers the fact that Meyer and Siegel had turned murder-for-hire into a lucrative practice. The fact that Meyer and Luciano together had been credited with successfully engineering the demise of the era's top "Mustache Petes" leaves open the real possibility that Meyer Lansky might have had a hand in the demise of others too. There was a great deal at stake besides the mere prestige of getting Schultz. Clearly these criminal entrepreneurs realized early that Prohibition wealth would soon dry up unless they hammered out new territories. The ensuing scramble to create and hold new ground made life as a gangster almost a contradiction in terms.

"Last year, according to police, there were 359 homicides in New York City. Of these, 22 are ascribed indisputably to gang warfare," the *New York Times* said. Gambling disputes were blamed for thirteen more. Officially, police classed fifty-three deaths as the result of unknown motives; unofficially, they readily admitted the strong possibility that most of these could be classed as gang murders. Although no one could prove it, the Bugs and Meyer gang excelled at carrying out just such activities. With Meyer to plan these hits and Siegel to carry them out, their success was all but assured. One thing was clear—a team like theirs never had to look very far for work. And who dared challenge them?

THE 1935 gangland toll reached at least one hundred. At this time a gang willing to do a volume business would be in securities, the policy slip and slot-machine industries, food markets, laundries, restaurants, many types of retail stores, smuggling alcohol, and the manufacturing of fake whiskey labels.

"The rackets are a substitute for bootlegging as an outlet for the energies of organized criminals," the *New York Times* said. Nothing was as lucrative as bootlegging whiskey during Prohibition, but added up, the many different rackets became a gold mine. That is why the new gang leader was not a specialist, but had his hand in many rackets at once.

None of this escaped the prosecutor Thomas Dewey, who repeatedly went before grand juries in attempts to stamp out organized crime rings in New York. But the bosses hid behind political and legal walls. Meyer Lansky continued his climb to the top of gangland circles.

With Schultz out of the way, gangland leaders knew they'd either have to fight for their lives and turf or be put permanently out of business. As the inevitable war began, several top-flight leaders emerged.

The rivals included Johnny Torrio, an old-time gangleader with interests in both New York and Chicago. Torrio had stepped down as a boss of Chicago mobs during Prohibition when Al Capone emerged as a powerful boss, and Torrio was left to concentrate on his New York holdings. Authorities said there were six other major gangs that included Luciano, Charles "Buck" Siegel, Meyer Lansky, Louis "Lepke" Buchalter, Jacob "Gurrah" Shapiro, and Abe "Longy" Zwillman of Newark.

"If the police theory of the Schultz-Amberg killings is correct, someone connected with the new combination engaged professional gunmen, probably hired assassins from some other city, to come to Newark to put these leaders out of the way and break up their gangs in order to prevent any interference with the plans of 'the Big Six' for a monopoly of the profitable policy, racing hand book rackets, labor trouble and other rackets of the metropolitan area," said the *Newark Evening News*.

An investigation prompted by a federal grand jury probe of organized crime in the fall of 1939 gave authorities a clearer picture of crime families in America. The investigation centered around persons believed to be harboring criminals indicted by New York authorities. It showed that criminals throughout the country sought by New York authorities were being hidden out in various parts of the country. Again, the name Meyer Lansky emerged among the leaders of major crime families.

The grand jury called Bugsy Siegel as a principal witness and a principal member of the Bugsy and Meyer mob shortly after Louis Lepke surrendered to authorities for questioning.

"They (Meyer and Siegel) were connected also with Lepke and his partner, Jacob 'Gurrah' Shapiro, Charles

'Lucky' Luciano and Joe Adonis of Brooklyn, the *New York Times* reported. "As early as 1931, the Bugs and Meyer gang began to extend its empire," the *Times* said. "While Lepke's interests were extended to Baltimore—as the grand jury determined—those of the Bugs-Meyer gang were extended to Philadelphia, Pittsburgh and Cleveland." Testimony showed that as Meyer's influence grew, he and Siegel set up shop in Los Angeles.

"The bosses themselves moved on," the grand jury was told, "where they suffered no diminution of the rich living scale they had enjoyed in New York." When Siegel emerged as a principal in various California enterprises, authorities sought to determine who had bankrolled these new ventures.

"The federal grand jury investigating the national crime set-up is keenly interested in the business affairs of Benjamin 'Bugsy' Siegel and has sought particularly to find out what persons have lent the former New York gang leader large sums of money." It was common knowledge that Siegel was sent to California by Meyer, although authorities could not prove it. Siegel, however, refused to cooperate with the grand jury, saying he had "forgotten where his finances had come from," and the investigation eventually ran out of steam.

In 1954, Lansky's name again emerged during a Senate investigation of underworld ties to military contracts. Senator John Williams said that the Truman administration's laxity made it possible for the underworld to successfully win a government contract related to military mobilization. Williams said that Louis Pokrass had won top-secret Army clearance in 1951. A few weeks later, it became known that Pokrass was a business partner with Lansky and Frank Costello. Later the same year, a business associate of Pokrass', Franklin Lamb, became an assistant to Charles Wilson, a former president of General Electric who was Defense Mobilization director at the time. Lamb won the appointment without the background check customarily done by the FBI on the recommendation of Maj. Gen. Harry Vaughan, military aide to President Truman. In this post, access to "advance information on all allocations of critical materials, the inauguration of rationing or price controls or other important actions would have a major effect on prices of key commodities in this country during the Korean War," it was reported.

"Mr. Lamb did not draw pay, but served from Sept. 4, 1951 through Oct. 24, 1951. At the same time, Lamb was paid by the Tele-King Company and was a stockholder in the firm in which Lansky, Costello and Joe Adonis were also invested.

"The story of underworld participation in his company, organized in 1947 as the Consolidated Television Corporation, was disclosed in February and March of 1951 in the testimony of Costello and Lansky before the Senate Crime Investigating Committee.

"During the Korean War, Senator Williams said, Tele-King Company obtained approximately $7 million in government contracts at prices averaging nearly 20 percent higher than other responsible bids." They also received substantial advance payments on contracts even after they had been turned down for bank loans necessary to fulfill the contracts. In effect, the government was bankrolling their bid with these advance payments. The Army later said that Pokrass' top-secret clearance had been an accident, saying their original intention was to only allow Tele-King a "secret" clearance to sensitive documents. The "secret" clearance was revoked in December of 1952.

In the 1970s, federal prosecutors made a serious attempt to get Meyer Lansky. Lansky ignored a grand jury subpoena and fled to Israel in 1970. He obtained a tourist visa and told Israeli authorites he intended to vacation there for at least four months. He took rooms at the Dan Hotel in Tel Aviv where he registered with his wife Thelma under his own name. When asked if he had been contacted by old associates since his arrival in Israel, Lansky replied "Associates? I haven't any associates. I'm my own associate."

The now-aging underworld figure, credited with making millions for the mob through its Las Vegas holdings and other enterprises, told a reporter who tracked him down at his hotel by phone that his reputation as an underworld figure had been greatly exaggerated over the years. "I was just made (into) something and that's all," he said. "I was made (into) something to make me salable. They gave me a title and that's it. So that's the way it goes. But I'm sure people that knew me knew who I am and what I am," he said, then abruptly ended the conversation by saying "thank you," and hanging up.

At the time it was alleged that Lansky had offered any country that would allow him to stay up to one million dollars in cash. Apparently there were no takers so he chose Israel.

After years of crime-related activities, it took until 1970 for the U.S. government to muster up enough evidence to go after him in a serious way. He invested millions in Israel while he attempted to claim Israeli citizenship under the Law of Return, which offers citizenship to anyone born of a Jewish mother. He proved an embarrassment to the Israeli government, however, which forced him to leave the country and return to the U.S.

He underwent open heart surgery in 1973, the same year the government slapped him with income tax evasion charges. On that charge, he was acquitted. In 1974, at the age of seventy-six, his contempt conviction in the grand jury matter was overturned on appeal. At the same time, a federal judge ordered the government to refrain from prosecuting Lansky because he was old and in failing health.

Lansky had again escaped unscathed.

In *America's Paychecks, Who Makes What,* author David Harrop said Lansky's personal wealth was in the neighborhood of between $100 and $300 million. No wonder Lansky could once say of the crime syndicate he had helped found, "We're bigger than U.S. Steel."

Meyer Lansky lived out his later years in a waterfront condo in Miami Beach instead of jail, and died in 1983 an unlikely death for a mobster. No shots were fired, no one was injured. Old age did what no rival could.

Chapter 8
Canaries Without Wings:
Abe "Kid Twist" Reles
and Joseph Valachi

AMONG the most notorious mob figures to emerge in the 1940s was Abe "Kid Twist" Reles, a professional killer from Brooklyn and a respected member of the feared Albert Anastasia bunch. By 1940, the Kid had been arrested at least forty times on various raps, including six murders, possession of drugs, robbery, and assault. He did time, but never much time, considering his line of work.

The Kid emerged as a leading gangland figure, not just for his crimes, but because he turned state's witness, or in street language, became a stoolie. Credited with having an almost photographic memory, the Kid rolled over on a couple of cronies after they were picked up and charged with the shooting death of a loan shark by the name of Whitey Rudnick. It wasn't just beating the rap for Whitey's murder that turned the Kid, it was fear that a far more sinister conspiracy would be revealed by one of his co-defendants. Only the first to rat could bargain for immunity.

It was a conspiracy that wiped away the police axiom that gangland violence was merely random and wanton. Bodies turned up almost daily in public landfills, especially in Brooklyn. Stiffs were found floating in New York's East River at least once a week, or dumped in the Hackensack Meadowlands over in Jersey. What authorities did not know or even suspect in the forties was the fact that most of these killings were systematically ordered and carried out by an internal Mafia police force known as Murder, Inc. "Kid Twist" was a soldier in this secret army of hitters. When he was picked up for Whitey's murder, he knew he had something valuable to trade. He decided to squeal about the inner workings of Murder, Inc. before any other defendant seized the opportunity. His testimony shook the very foundation of underworld activities and in one broad sweep cleared up nearly fifty recent murders in Brooklyn alone. Murder, Inc. turf, however, spread across the country. Reles' astounding testimony shed light on dozens of other unsolved killings which he offered details about murders the authorities knew nothing about.

Abe Reles' revelations made him the most notorious canary in crime history. He held that title for the next twenty years, until the appearance of Joseph Valachi, The King of Song, another mobster whose name became synonymous with "rat."

Murder, Inc. was the syndicate's squad of professional killers in the decade between 1930 and 1940. It wasn't an entirely novel idea in underworld circles, where similar gangs had existed in this country as far back as the nineteenth century, but its national scope was unprecedented.

The discovery of the infamous Murder Stable in New

York City in 1901 revealed the existence of a "Mafia" or a "Black Hand" operating in this country. That year, the U.S. Secret Service began investigating a supposed anarchist plot to assassinate President William McKinley. New York detective Joseph Petrosino was part of the investigation, during the course of which he and the Secret Service discovered the so-called Murder Stable, a property located in Italian Harlem at 323 East 107th Street.

Digging under the floor, they found the remains of sixty murder victims. It became clear that the victims had been killed during an Italian war for control of the waterfront. Joseph Petrosino, the victim of a hit himself when he went to Italy to investigate underworld activity firsthand, was the subject of a popular sixties film, *Pay or Die*. With the discovery of the Murder Stable, the existence of organized crime and organized murder became a ghoulish reality.

Organized murder wasn't just the specialty of Italian gangs either. The existence of these mercenary squads crossed racial and ethnic boundaries. Their hitmen worked for anyone. In some instances these freelancers had printed price lists for their services, which ranged from five dollars to convince a borrower to pay a loan shark, to one hundred dollars for a simple killing.

Murder, Inc., however, was formed in Brooklyn as an arm of the powerful gangs controlled by the Italian, Jewish, and Irish mob in New York run by Lucky Luciano, Meyer Lansky, and others during Prohibition. When booze was legalized, Murder, Inc. remained intact, its sole purpose being the enforcement of negotiated turf treaties between various gangs. Like a corporation, each gang negotiated a market share of the prostitution, loan-sharking, gambling, racketeering, and narcotics business in the city. While agreeing to respect each other's turf, not everyone kept their word. Murder, Inc. was used as a deterrent, which didn't always work.

When a Murder, Inc. representative did a job, it was commonly referred to as "just business." Unlike the hit squads that had preceded it, Murder, Inc. was never used for personal or political reasons. It was strictly a business expense, and as gangster Bugsy Siegel once said, "We only kill each other."

Anastasia was the so-called Lord High Executioner. Louis Lepke, a powerful labor insider, acted as a high-ranking board member. Whenever a potential hit was commissioned, it could not proceed without the approval of various underworld bosses around the country, including the likes of Frank Costello, Bugsy Siegel, Lucky Luciano, Meyer Lansky, or Moe Dalitz, who headed the mob in Cleveland.

The soldiers who worked directly beneath Anastasia and Lepke were Abe "Kid Twist" Reles and the likes of Vito "Chicken Head" Guarino, "Blue Jaw" Magoon, Happy Maione, "Dasher" Abbandano, Bugsy Goldstein, and the ruthless Pittsburgh Phil Strauss.

Each soldier had a special talent. "Chicken Head" perfected his aim by shooting the heads off live chickens. Bugsy Goldstein's tool of choice was the garrote. Pittsburgh Phil seemed to be the most accomplished among his colleagues, credited with committing between fifty and a hundred murders single-handedly. The squad hung out at a candy store in the Brownsville section of Brooklyn called Midnight Rose's.

When a hit was ordered, the word was passed along through underlings. Like military soldiers, the squad went wherever they were told, usually assigned to kill a perfect stranger.

Many believed that Murder, Inc. did in Dutch Schultz, one of the most famous members of modern organized crime in the United States. In 1935, prosecutor Thomas Dwwey was after Schultz. The mobster responded with a demand that Dewey be killed. This violated the basic rule that no politicians were to be clipped, and no personal laundry was to be aired. When Schultz's demand was rejected, he went away to do the job himself. A mob contract went out on Schultz to stop him.

When Schultz was killed in Newark in the fall of 1935, authorities speculated it was a result of a turf war with one of the New York gang factions. When questioned about his killers, Schultz died without telling what he must have known, that he was a victim of Murder, Inc., not the greed of a rival.

FIVE years after Schultz was killed, Abe Reles was picked up in connection with the brutal killing of Whitey Rudnick. Rudnick had been strangled and stabbed at least sixty times, and his skull had been fractured.

"Whitey got it because he was a stool pigeon," Reles told Brooklyn District Attorney William O'Dwyer. His words were both ironic and prophetic. For more than a year, the Kid fingered his associates, implicating them in some 200 murders. In total, he said the national syndicate had committed between 400 and 500 murders in the decade beginning in 1930.

Pittsburgh Phil was nailed for at least one hundred of these alone. Bugsy Goldstein was convicted for the killing of gambler Puggy Feinstein. Both men eventually went to the electric chair. Mendy Weiss, Louis Capone (no relation to Alphonse), Frank "The Dasher" Abbandando, and Happy Maione were also executed. The highest-ranking member, Louis Lepke, was himself convicted of murder and executed. The only remaining kingpin was Anastasia himself, the Lord High Executioner.

Squad member Charlie Workman, charged with the Schultz killing, saw the handwriting on the wall. He pleaded guilty and got life instead of the chair. The Kid's testimony was having a devastating effect on "The Company."

Naturally, the authorities tried to hide Reles well. Unfortunately, they chose the sixth floor wing of the Half Moon Hotel in the Coney Island section of Brooklyn, where he was heavily guarded around the clock by police officers. In November 1941, Abe "Kid Twist" Reles literally took a dive out of the sixth-floor window of his hotel room. He either jumped, fell, or was thrown out, and his police guard somehow missed the event. Tied sheets were found hanging outside the window, giving the impression that the Kid had tried to climb down, but they weren't long enough to do the job. The theories that he simply fell failed to explain why his body was found some twenty feet out from the building. It was more likely that he was thrown, but by whom?

"As long as Abe Reles was alive, we had a perfectly good case against Albert Anastasia. But the day Reles went through that window and was killed, that particular case, for want of corroboration, was no longer a clear case," said O'Dwyer. "When I left the army [in 1942], Murder, Inc. in Brooklyn was completely and utterly destroyed." George Beldock, who succeeded

O'Dwyer as Brooklyn District Attorney, however, said that office files indicated that O'Dwyer had given orders to halt the investigation of the Brooklyn waterfront. O'Dwyer denied the charge, saying there was no statute of limitation on murder charges. In another attack, O'Dwyer was accused of being "on friendly terms" with such gangland luminaries as Frank Costello, Joe Adonis, and Irving Sherman.

O'Dwyer's case against Anastasia depended on the Kid's testimony, and he eventually withdrew. Ultimately, a Brooklyn grand jury charged O'Dwyer with "negligence, incompetence and flagrant irresponsibility," which statement immediately drew fire from the prosecutor, who had otherwise dealt the mob a significant blow. Murder, Inc. appeared to be out of commission, but mob activities continued unabated, including the murders of members who got out of line.

The grand jury said O'Dwyer could have continued his prosecution because he was "in possession of competent legal evidence that Anastasia was guilty of first degree murder and other vicious crimes." The proof supposedly was enough to serve up Anastasia's indictment, but the case was dropped.

Meanwhile, the investigation into the Kid's death continued on and off for ten years. In the ensuing years, the Mafia's business was repeatedly aired in a public forum. It again surfaced in a major way in the fall of 1945, when O'Dwyer made a successful run in the New York mayoral race as the Democratic candidate. The Republicans used the grand jury presentment, criticizing O'Dwyer in an attempt to paint him at best as being soft on criminals or, at worst, corrupt.

"I am today in exactly the same state of mind towards gangsters and the underworld that I was in

1940," O'Dwyer said during a radio broadcast on station WNYC. "I want to give [the underworld] a message now, if they are here they had better pack up and get out fast, because when I go in as mayor of the city of New York it will be just as hot for them in 1946 as it was in Brooklyn in 1940. They will travel the same trail that led others to the electric chair," candidate O'Dwyer said. Citing his record, he said his staff had solved fifty murders in Brooklyn and eleven others in various other parts of the country, according to a *New York Times* story during the campaign.

Beldock criticized O'Dwyer for allowing Anastasia to avoid prosecution. He said O'Dwyer still had an opportunity to present evidence to the grand jury, which was in session. Anastasia was accused of killing Peter Panto and running rackets along New York's waterfront. Beldock, denying that his comments were an attack on O'Dwyer, said his files still contained the strong evidence gathered by O'Dwyer's staff when he was the Brooklyn district attorney.

O'Dwyer was informally asked to appear before the same grand jury that had criticized him five years earlier in the Anastasia investigation. Beldock linked Costello and Adonis to Anastasia through their waterfront operations. The names of underworld figures surfaced in daily stories during the campaign. Many of these previously anonymous kingpins in underworld activities had come aboveground through no fault of their own. It was the legacy left them by Abe "Kid Twist" Reles.

IN 1963, Abe "Kid Twist" lost his title as the most celebrated singer in crime history when a low-level member of a Cosa Nostra crime family began an amazing song. Joseph Valachi, a three-time loser doing time in a federal penitentiary in Atlanta for murder and narcotics trafficking, decided to sing before the Senate Permanent Investigations Subcommittee, chaired by Senator John L. McClellan. His material made the front page of the *Sunday Washington Star* and subsequently became a widely sold autobiography and a made-for-television movie.

Valachi had been a soldier in the underworld family of Salvatore Maranzano. In 1931, Maranzano was killed, allegedly by members of the Lucky Luciano group. Valachi wisely changed his allegiance and went to work for Luciano, where he became an enforcer, a drug pusher, and a sometime hit man. In 1959, he was convicted on federal narcotics charges and sentenced to fifteen to twenty years in prison.

Valachi was in prison with Don Vito Genovese, who had been convicted on trumped-up drug charges and sentenced to fifteen years in prison. From the pen Don Vito continued to oversee his empire. Someone apparently told Don Vito that Joe Valachi was a rat. Unfortunately, at that time, the charge was untrue. Valachi later claimed that "Don Vito gave me the kiss of death in our cell." While dramatic, the tale is a little hard to swallow.

In any case, Valachi had become a poor insurance risk. For some reason, Valachi believed his killer would be one Joe DiPalermo. When innocently approached by another man, Joseph Saupp, the excitable Valachi beat him to death with an iron pipe. He was subsequently convicted of murder and resentenced to life. Then he decided to roll over on his former associates in return for federal protection.

The sixty-year-old Valachi soon appeared before the McClellan subcommittee in Washington. Chain-smoking and speaking in a gruff, hoarse whiskey voice, Valachi painted a lurid picture of the so-called Mafia. He identified Don Vito as the nation's leading crime boss, even though he was still doing time. He went on to name at least 317 top members of the organization, and pinpointed many of their activities with some accuracy. Guarded by some 200 U.S. marshals, Valachi's testimony was considered significant by former U.S. Attorney General Robert F. Kennedy, but often dismissed by government skeptics as being just good theater put on by a desperate man with nothing to lose.

However, Valachi's testimony shed new light on various activities that had previously been shrouded in secrecy. Perhaps the most significant thing Valachi's testimony offered authorities was an updated list of who's who in organzied crime. Valachi said that Don Vito Genovese headed what was known in gangland circles as "the Commission," even from his cell in Atlanta.

The Commission was comprised of bosses who headed various crime families in key cities around the country. Each family controlled vice, gambling, narcotics, numbers, and prostitution activities in designated territories, and the Commission decided which families controlled which activities or territories. It also judged any disputes that arose.

Valachi said there were powerful groups operating in New York, Detroit, Philadelphia, Chicago, New Orleans, Buffalo, Miami, Kansas City, St. Louis, Cleveland, Los Angeles, San Francisco, Providence, Boston, and parts of New Jersey. The mob organized, franchised, and peddled murder and vice in much the same way McDonald's would later sweep across the country selling hamburgers and fresh fries.

In November of 1957, Valachi said, the Commission met at a house in Apalachin, New York. Authorities already knew the meeting had taken place. The Feds were able to surprise dozens of powerful mob figures that day. Members of the Commission, who had mistakenly believed they were meeting secretly in a safe house of a member, fled in all directions as agents raided the place. Some sixty well-known mobsters were brought in for questioning, but no one ever found out the purpose of the meeting. Years later, Valachi claimed the convention had brought together at least 110 top syndicate bosses from around the country. It had been called by Don Vito to reorganize and streamline mob activities. Don Vito also wanted the Commission's clearance to hit Frank Costello and Albert Anastasia. Like a corporate board meeting, the Commission was planning to cut some 200 members from their joint payroll "because they were no longer usefull."

Valachi said the organization operated according to a strict code of silence, *omerta*. He said members took loyalty oaths, which included blood rituals and death threats aimed at any member who betrayed another. Their "families" were tied together in much the same way wealthy families and royalty had been aligned for centuries, through arranged marriages and common interest.

In 1969, Joe Valachi published his memoirs, entitled *The Valachi Papers*. The "Cosa Nostra" delighted J. Edgar Hoover, who had previously believed that there was no such thing as the Mafia. Now, Hoover insisted that his men had been on to the mob all along.

Without a doubt, Valachi's testimony hurt and damaged many Mafiosi. It hurt the Genovese family for certain and prompted a new internal power struggle. When Valachi's testimony ended, "he became the most carefully guarded inmate in the federal prison system." Moved repeatedly from prison to prison, he was finally confined in the La Tuna Federal Correction Institution at El Paso, Texas, where he died on April 3, 1971. He would have been about sixty-eight years old. Nevertheless, historical references to his demise include the widely held suspicion that reports of his death were "a con to let the Feds hide him on the outside."

Chapter 9
Hands-On Hollywood Hotshot:
Benjamin "Bugsy" Siegel

When the creator of Las Vegas
gambling crapped out....

WHEN Harry Greenberg, known to underworld cronies as Big Greenie, was sentenced to death by the syndicate in New York, he fled west to California, hoping to escape the wrath of his mob bosses.

The job of getting Big Greenie fell to Ben Siegel, known behind his back as Bugsy. Bugsy, a New Yorker who raised hell on the Lower East Side as the pal of the feared Meyer Lansky, had been well-schooled in the arts of running gambling operations, stealing cars, and bootlegging. By 1920, the so-called Bugs-Meyer outfit routinely hijacked booze shipments for fun and profit until it occurred to them there was more money in hiring out their services to protect the same shipments they had been boosting. Murder was also something Bugsy did well. He was alleged to have been one of the enthusiastic gunmen in Murder, Inc.

During the Roaring Twenties, there emerged a brand of gangster who put the business of gambling, racketeering, prostitution, and narcotics ahead of personal feuds. It was through this alliance that Siegel and Lansky began doing important jobs for the rising stars in the Italian mob, including such powerful men as Lucky Luciano, Joe Adonis, and Frank Costello. The Bugs and Meyer Gang often provided the muscle to carry out Luciano's ambitious schemes as he moved against rivals in a push to wipe out old time Mafia bosses like Salvatore Maranzano and Giuseppe "Joe The Boss" Masseria.

It was often said that Bugsy favored murder the way a tradesman prefers certain jobs over others. In the vernacular of the underworld, Siegel was considered a "cowboy." A prosecutor familiar with the mobster was quoted in the Los Angeles newspapers: "This is the way the boys have of describing a man who is not satisfied to frame a murder but actually has to be in on the kill in person." That was allegedly the case in the 1931 hit of Joe The Boss, gunned down during a lunch with Luciano ion Brooklyn. In fact, the hit was arranged by Luciano, who conveniently left the table long enough for Bugsy and three other gunmen to pump six bullets into "Joe The Boss" Masseria, ending an era of violence that had begun decades before.

Luciano, Costello, and other mobsters realized there were profits enough for everyone, as long as members of various gangs remained under the control of their bosses. A deal was struck between the various ethnic gangs—Italians, Jews, and Irish—which prompted the establishment of a nationwide crime syndicate.

Initially, Bugsy was assigned the duties of a hit man, carrying out numerous murders as the syndicate gained control of wealthy gangland empires in cities across the country. While killing foes came as easy to Bugsy as boosting trucks had in the early days, he found an even more comfortable niche when the syndicate sent him to the West Coast to run their Los Angeles gambling business.

In a short time. Bugsy charmed his way into Hollywood circles, hobnobbing with the likes of Clark Gable, Gary Cooper. Jean Harlow, and other Hollywood luminaries. A New York smoothie, Bugsy soon convinced these rich and famous people to invest in a number of his con schemes.

Often Bugsy disappeared from a lavish party to go on a hit, as happened when he got the call to kill Big Greenie. It was 1939, and Greenie's hit was carried out along with Frankie Carbo and a member of the national hitman's squad known as Murder, Inc., Allie Tannenbaum. When the Big Greenie hit was over, Bugsy returned to the party he had been attending and, as some said, he continued to ''charm the panties'' off an array of Hollywood starlets there that night.

In the fall of that year, Bugsy was hauled in front of a grand jury that was keenly interested in his business affairs. The panel wanted to know the names of anyone who loaned Siegel large sums of money.

This marked his third time before a grand jury. Each time, Bugsy steadfastly refused to disclose the financial details of his businesses.

A few days later, on September 29, 1939, Siegel again refused to answer questions concerning the whereabouts of Louis Lepke. This time, however, a federal judge ordered him jailed until he could remember the last time he had seen Lepke. The judge ruled that Siegel's memory lapse was ''frivolous and contumacious.'' He had been . ordered to appear in federal court after he failed to answer similar questions before the grand jury. Little seemed to instill fear in Bugsy Siegel. A trip to Europe during World War II supports that theory.

"He and one of his mistresses, Countess Dorothy DiFrasso, trekked to Italy to sell Benito Mussolini a revolutionary explosive device," according to one published account of the incident. "While staying on the DiFrasso estate, Siegel met top Nazi officials Hermann Goering and Joseph Goebbels. According to underworld legend, Bugsy took an instant dislike to the pair for personal reasons and might well have killed them had not the countess intervened."

It was just one of the many stories that circulated about Siegel, illustrating his predilection for violence and mayhem. However, Siegel and Lansky were considered brilliant gangsters, who in many ways were ahead of their time. It was the Lansky-Siegel connection that allowed other factions of crime families to merge for common causes. Together, they set the pattern for mob involvement in so-called "legitimate" enterprises. Lansky and Siegel had been partners since their teenage days on the Lower East Side, and they remained close until the end. When time ran out for Siegel, ironically, it was Lansky who was instrumental in hammering the final nails in his coffin. But in their heyday, the Siegel-Lansky team was smooth and powerful.

They were at least partly responsible for establishing Las Vegas as a gambling mecca. The idea first occurred to Siegel when he and Lansky moved their operations to California. Siegel wanted his mob partners to invest six million dollars in the construction of the first luxury hotel in Las Vegas, the Flamingo. Siegel had been placed in charge of the West Coast gambling operations, and the idea of creating a gambling empire in the desert town was itself an enormous gamble at the time. During World War II, Vegas was a backwater town with a few flytrap diners, gas stations, and some slot machine joints. Siegel, however, believed it was the natural location, since gambling was legal in Nevada. Reno was always popular with the syndicate, and Siegel had little trouble convincing his long-time partner to advance him the money needed to build the Flamingo, named for Siegel's girlfriend Virginia Hill, whose nickname was Flamingo. Virginia had a long history with the mob, having dated the likes of Frank Nitti, Frank Costello, and the man whom many said became her true love, Bugsy Siegel.

Although it was the first of many successful gambling operations in Vegas, the Flamingo was a financial disaster when it was built in the late 1940s. It failed in part, however, because the syndicate believed that Bugsy had skimmed money from the original six million dollars in construction funds. Once it was built, the hotel consistently lost money, and the mob demanded that Bugsy pay back the money or suffer the consequences. It is entirely possible that Siegel overestimated his influence and clout with Lansky, rumored to be among the top bosses in the syndicate, and able to approve a hit. Chiseling the mob's money was certainly reason enough to warrant a contract. However, Siegel believed a hit would never be ordered on him as long as Lansky sat on the Commission. He miscalculated.

In December 1946, the Commission met in Havana in an attempt to solve some problems among its members. Luciano had been deported to Italy, and there was serious rivalry between Vito Genovese and Frank Costello. Both believed they should fill Luciano's shoes as head of the Commission. Luciano arrived in Havana from Italy, hoping to hole up there until he could bribe his way back into the United States.

While this was the main reason for the meeting, another item on the agenda was Siegel's apparent disregard of warnings to return the mob's money. "Siegel had squandered huge sums of money building a great financial lemon," it had been reported. Ironically, it was Lansky's motion that brought the subject of Siegel's murder to the table.

"There's only one thing to do with a thief who steals from his friends. Benny's got to be hit," Lansky was quoted as saying. "I have no other choice."

Six months later, at midnight on June 20, Siegel was sitting in the living room of his $500,000 mansion in Beverly Hills. Virginia Hill was away in Europe on syndicate business. Siegel was with Allen Smiley, an associate, Mrs. Hill's brother, Charles, and Jerri Mason, a secretary.

"The killer, screened by shrubbery, crept up the driveway of the adjoining house and fired an Armytype carbine through a trellis only a few yards from where Siegel sat," the *New York Times* later reported. "Neighbors heard the shots and reported that a car roared down the street a few seconds later."

Nine shots came through a window, three of them hitting Siegel in the head. He died instantly. His death at the hands of his long-time associates was ironic in many ways. When he was building the Flamingo, he allegedly told construction millionaire Del Webb that working for the mob was safe because "we only kill each other."

Whether or not Webb believed him is not known. It was said that Bugsy Siegel was simultaneously the most colorful, the most charming, and the most fiery-tempered of all syndicate mob killers.

Chapter 10
Bumped Up the River—
The Bloodless Hit:
Vito Genovese

MAFIA kingpin Vito Genovese, the self-proclaimed underworld "Boss of All Bosses," died quietly in a federal prison hospital of a heart ailment in 1969. While no shots were fired and no bloody carnage accompanied his departure at the age of seventy-one, you could say his friends were largely responsible for getting rid of him in a bloodless coup that put him behind bars for the rest of his life.

The truth of the matter was that Genovese, despite the empire he ruled, even from behind bars, just wasn't as tricky as the mobsters who engineered his fall with the grateful help of federal investigators.

Even long after the scheme that eventually put Don Vito away was over, he didn't realize it had been his underworld friends who arranged it, not the federal authorities who prosecuted him.

It was the ambitious Genovese who had engineered Frank Costello's eventual retirement. By most accounts, it was he who ordered the hit on Frank in the lobby of his Central Park West apartment building in the late 1950s. But Costello survived the shooting attack, then showed how much class he really had by refusing to identify his attacker. Costello was a team player, even if the team he was on played a brand of hardball that could have ended his posh life. Costello knew the attack was a business liability. It was an inter-gang affair, not the business of the authorities who'd lock up for life anyone who wore a fedora if they had their way.

Genovese was a general intent upon winning as much mob-controlled territory as possible. The easiest, most efficient way to do that was to simply kill off the opposition.

Like toy soldiers, they fell one by one beginning in the late 1950s, when Lucky Luciano was deported back to Italy. He had planned to hole up in Cuba until the heat from the Feds subsided, but deportation squelched his plans. Luciano was out of touch.

Joe Adonis was about to suffer the same fate because he was too busy fending off authorities investigating his activities to pay much attention to mob business. The government was using tax laws to get Costello.

After the botched attempt on his life, Frank knew his days were numbered if he stayed active. No one was safe from Genovese's campaign to run the syndicate single-handedly. Even Albert Anastasia, known as the Lord High Executioner, had been pushed aside by assassins' bullets. He knew it was only a matter of time until he suffered the same fate. Costello moved swiftly to get himself out of harm's way by making several deft moves.

Publicly he made it known that he wanted to retire. Secretly, he engineered a scheme along with Meyer

Lansky, Lucky Luciano, and Carlo Gambino to hand Genovese to the Feds. Genovese had taken over drug territories in several locations. Once his influence was firmly confirmed in various drug operations, federal prosecutors wound up with damning evidence that eventually sent him up the river for life.

He was convicted in 1959 and died in jail ten years later. Ironically, Costello himself was jailed in Atlanta where Genovese was serving his time, and it is alleged the two kingpins reconciled their differences.

A profile of Genovese emerged a year after his death in wiretapped conversations obtained by federal investigators investigating crime activities in New Jersey. Although he had died quietly in prison, authorities had known for decades that he had ordered the executions of scores of other men. Early in 1970, transcripts of wiretap conversations released by the FBI implicated Genovese in the death of Anthony "Tony Bender" Strollo in 1962.

Strollo had been a major Mafia figure from New Jersey who suddenly dropped out of sight in 1962. "It had been widely believed and confirmed in the transcript that Strollo was killed on orders of Vito Genovese," one newspaper account said. Strollo was said to have controlled the underworld's bar and night club operations on New York's East Side and in Greenwich Village. "His fate has been a matter of conjecture since he walked out of his Fort Lee, New Jersey, mansion one April evening in 1962 and disappeared. His body was never found," the story said.

A telephone call made a year later by one Anthony "Little Pussy" Russo, a reputed captain of the Genovese crime family, gave the Feds the information that linked his disappearance to Genovese. Little Pussy was talking to Angelo "Gyp" DeCarlo. When DeCarlo got busted in a loan-sharking–extortion case, a federal judge said those taped conversations could be made public although they were considered "hearsay" testimony and could not be used as evidence. In that tape, Russo relates details of an earlier conversation he had had with mobster Ruggiero "Richie The Boot" Boiardo, another high-ranking New Jersey mobster. On one tape, Genovese is identified as the man who ordered the Strollo hit. But the 1,200-page FBI transcripts also provided a valuable road map to the mob and the politicians they controlled, many of them tied directly to high-ranking mobsters, including Genovese.

Those tapes were akin to listening to a Sesame Street jingle compared to the crimes Genovese had been linked to over the years.

The *Times* said "Vito Genovese's throne, from which he rules as 'Boss of All Bosses' in the New York area, rested on the coffins of several predecessors . . ." The *New York Times* was suggesting what underworld figures all knew—that Genovese had ordered the death of anyone who opposed his ascent to the throne.

Genovese reportedly ran his family from prison. Even within the joint, Genovese wielded considerable clout, exercising the right to choose his own cell mates, among other things. He served time in the Atlanta Penitentiary and was later transferred to Leavenworth in the Midwest, where he continued to reign.

Born near Naples in the town of Rosiglione, Italy, in the fall of 1897, Genovese arrived in the United States at the age of fifteen. His family settled in New York in the Little Italy section. His crime career began with pushcart holdups. He ran errands for the Old-World Mafia dons and was later promoted to bag man, making collections for their various operations. In no time, he became a rising star along with Salvatore Luciania, who was later called Charlie "Lucky" Luciano.

Genovese's street exploits earned him the title of Don Vitone. Both Genovese and Luciano were cunning and smart, and believed to have been responsible, at least in part, for the undoing of their boss, Giuseppe "The Boss" Masseria. They betrayed Masseria to make way for Salvatore Maranzano, who aspired to become "The Boss of All Bosses." After Masseria got it in a Coney Island restaurant, Maranzano tried to take over.

"Maranzano's dream of empire was short-lived. He was murdered less than six months after Masseria," the *New York Times* said, naming Genovese and Luciano. By 1931, Genovese had earned widespread respect in mob circles, in part because of his associations with some of the most powerful underworld figures in New York. That respect also came from the suspicion that he, too, had been responsible for thinning their ranks with deft violence. He was believed to have ordered the deaths of Willie Moretti in 1951, Steve Franse in 1953, and Albert Anastasia in 1957. His taste for violence did not stop with high-ranking mobsters. He could wield his power downward, striking out at anyone who prevented him from having the things he wanted to own—even women.

His wife died in 1931. There is a legend that a short time later, Genovese fell in love with a neighbor, Anna Petillo, who had nursed Mrs. Genovese in her final days. Unfortunately, Anna had a husband, but Vito soon took care of that problem. "The body of Mr. Petillo, dead by strangulation, was found today on a roof," the *Daily News* reported. "Don Vito and the widow Petillo were united in marriage twelve days later.''

Don Vito wore expensive, tailor-made suits and was often seen in New York night clubs. He lived in a small five-room house in Atlantic Highlands, New Jersey, with his first wife. With Anna Petillo, he upgraded his lifestyle, moving into a huge mansion. His New Jersey neighbors viewed him as a successful businessman. Few of them knew they lived next door to one of the most notorious gangsters in the history of American crime. When his relationship with his second wife soured, the true nature of his business was revealed in open court by his soon-to-be ex-wife. She described him as a thug whose large income came mostly from breaking the backs of his victims and through his widespread control of night clubs and gambling activities in New York.

It was easy to see how neighbors could believe this well-dressed man was just another successful businessman. ''Realizing as early as 1925 that a legitimate business could be a cover for illegal operations as well as a source of income, he set up the Genovese Trading Company, handling waste paper and tags,'' it was reported. ''Gradually, he expanded his legitimate business along with his rackets.'' Subsequent investigations by various authorities showed how integral these ''legitimate'' businesses had been. In the summer of 1967, crime statistics revealed that the Genovese and Gambino crime families controlled ninety percent of the garbage business in Westchester County, New York.

The owner of a luncheonette, who asked to remain anonymous, said charges for removing his garbage went from eight dollars to one hundred dollars a month in two years after new owners acquired the company which had previously hauled his refuse.

"I complained once that I couldn't afford another price boost," the man said. "They said if I couldn't make out, I should burn the store down. If they cut you off, you can't get another company to take away your waste. You might as well get out of the business then," he added.

It was tactics like these that became the focus of a federal investigation that same summer. The Feds were looking into a variety of operations, including night clubs, restaurants, and bars suspected as being fronts for Genovese crime family members. In newspaper accounts, Genovese was considered only a titular leader when in fact, he still had considerable clout, even though he was behind bars at the time. The Feds believed his lieutenants controlled numerous businesses in White Plains, Yonkers, and various other towns near New York.

When Maranzano was eliminated, Luciano took over, with Genovese acting as his underboss. While Luciano had no known desire to become the new "Boss of All Bosses," he still headed the largest of the five New York crime families. Meanwhile, Genovese moved quickly to take over as much of the illegal narcotics trafficking as possible. He ruled with an iron fist, willing to "off" soldiers under his command for the sightest infraction. Their fates were sealed if he uncovered any evidence they might be skimming profits from any of his operations.

The swift killing of Ferdinand "The Shadow" Boccia, who had the audacity to try to skim profits, almost brought Genovese himself down, and he had to leave the country in 1934. Back home in Italy with $750,000 in cash, he donated a quarter of a million to Benito Mussolini, the Fascist dictator. Genovese became the chief drug supplier for Count Ciano, Mussolini's foreign minister and son-in-law. Even from abroad, Genovese was credited with ordering the execution of a Mussolini detractor and long-time foe, newspaper editor Carlo Tresca. That hit was allegedly carried out by a Genovese underling at the time, Carlo Gambino, during Genovese's exile. When Mussolini fell, Genovese became an interpreter in 1944 for the Army Intelligence Service and somehow endeared himself to U.S. military forces in Europe. He became an expert at finding and exposing black market operatives in southern Italy. What the military didn't realize until much later was that Genovese didn't put these operations out of business, he just took over. Getting rid of the competition was one of the ways in which he would accumulate power in the U.S. He practiced the technique in Italy by disrupting the trade of black marketeers, then taking over their small businesses. In this way, he became a major player in the sale and distribution of black market gasoline. That scam came to an abrupt halt, however, when military intelligence identified him as a fugitive wanted in the U.S. for the Boccia murder.

He was extradited back to New York to stand trial for murder. But Genovese was on familiar ground in Brooklyn. The star witness against him, Peter LaTempa, was being held in protective custody, however his body was found before the start of the trial. LaTempa had been fatally poisoned, and the charges against Genovese were dismissed for lack of evidence.

While he was away, the order of things had changed drastically. Luciano was in jail, and Frank Costello had taken over.

"Genovese's return home did not bring his automatic restoration to the family throne," the *New York Times* said. "He began a whispering campaign to undercut Costello. Then, he arranged to get Costello out of the way by having him shot. The gunman bungled the job and Costello escaped with a superficial head wound. Suspecting Albert Anastasia . . . of an alliance with Costello, Genovese allegedly engineered Anastasia's murder."

Vito Genovese felt the world was too small for himself, Albert Anastasia, and the "retired" Frank Costello. Carlo Gambino, Anastasia's underboss, was known to be ambitious, and if Big Al could be removed from the scene, Gambino could take over. Finding the prospect attractive, Gambino reputedly contacted Joseph Profaci, and Profaci passed the word along to Joey Gallo. Big Al got it in the Park Sheraton barbershop.

Seeing the handwriting on the wall, Costello stepped aside and Don Vito settled into his place as head of the largest Mafia family in the country.

In a way, Genovese's coronation became a public affair when Mafia bosses from around the country gathered in Apalachin, New York shortly after Anastasia's murder. Their meeting was a disaster: The state police raided it and took dozens of leading Mafia dons into custody.

Genovese missed the fact that the meeting had been sabotaged by clever enemies like Costello, Luciano, Lansky, and Gambino, the heir to the Anastasia family. Gambino and Lansky had cooperated with Genovese to hit Anastasia so Gambino could gain power. Lansky wanted to eliminate the pressure Anastasia was putting on him for a share of the vast Cuban gambling profits.

The Apalachin meeting was interrupted before the

mobsters could conduct all the business planned for this
historic get-together. One item to be discussed involved
getting out of the narcotics business altogether. Too
many soldiers were being busted by local, state, and
federal authorities. The order to halt narcotics trafficking came from the Mafia's twelve-man national
commission. Although Genovese was one of the commissioners, the raid was timely for Genovese's purposes because he had recently financed a large drug
smuggling operation.

Genovese aspired to head the crime commission, but
he faced stiff competition. Still at the top were Costello, Lansky, Luciano, and Gambino. They could have
ordered him killed, but they devised a subtler plan.
They realized that an interfamily war would be senseless. So they plotted to get rid of Genovese another
way. They first set him up for a federal drug bust, but
the narcotics agents blew the opportunity and Genovese
slipped away. The underworld conspirators then
arranged a trap that took government incompetence into
account. The four paid a minor dope pusher named
Nelson Cantellops $100,000 to implicate Genovese in
a deal. Although it was strange that an unimportant
street pusher like Cantellops would have the type of
inside information to hang a don like Genovese, the
government gladly accepted his testimony to put Genovese away for the last time.

Further light on Don Vito's activities came in the
sensational Senate hearings in 1963 in which star witness Joe Valachi snitched on the mob. Valachi said
Genovese had repeatedly tried without success to
impose his will on gangsters who belonged to the organization of Joseph Profaci and Joe Bananas. When

asked to estimate Genovese's wealth, Valachi said he didn't know, but indicated that the "boss" was cheap.

"He wouldn't go for anything," Valachi said. for example, the Cosa Nostra, which once charged as much as $40,000 for members to join, stopped accepting new soldiers in 1958. This was obvious nonsense, as was much else of his "testimony," but there was enough truth in it to make it interesting.

Valachi said that Genovese, Lucky Luciano, and Ciro Terranova lured their boss Joe Masseria to a restaurant where they shot him to death. Terranova was assigned to drive the getaway car, but in Valachi's words "was shaking as he put the key in the ignition, so they had to remove him."

Valachi testified further that Genovese's rise in the organization was almost halted when he narrowly escaped being killed by Salvatore Maranzano some time after 1931. Maranzano had invited Luciano and Genovese to his Park Avenue office, where he planned to kill them both. However, another plot was carried out before they arrived. "Four Jews," Valachi said, "who posed as cops got there first and killed Maranzano." The gunmen were identified as racketeers who worked for mob leader Meyer Lansky.

Later in jail, Genovese openly complained to a fellow inmate about his conviction. "They gave me a bum rap," he was quoted as saying. "I got a bum rap in the narcotics case. I wouldn't have minded if they got me on income tax evasion because that would be fair."

Probably for the first time, some authorities agreed with Genovese. New York police labeled Valachi's testimony "bullshit" and described the sixty-year-old hood as a "small, publicity-loving bum."

Afterward, Genovese allegedly ordered a cell mate

of Valachi, Joe DiPalermo, to execute him. Valachi, in a frenzy of fear when approached by Joseph Saupp, beat the innocent man to death. He later turned state's evidence and told a fascinating, if perhaps fanciful, story about the Mafia in America.

Ironically, Genovese's jail cell complaints echoed more truth about those trying to put him away than he may have realized at the time. He died before federal authorities could tag him with the actual crimes they suspected he had committed.

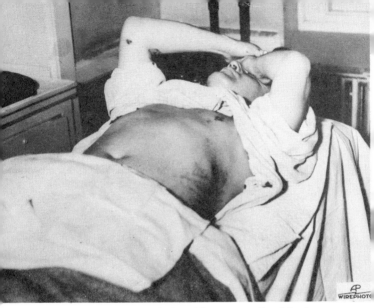

Dutch Schultz clutches his head in agony after his shooting in 1935. Note the wounds in the chest and right arm.

The body of Bugsy Siegel slumps on the divan after he was shot through the window on June 20, 1947.

November 12, 1941: Police gather around the body of "Kid Twist" Reles. He fell from the sixth floor of this Coney Island hotel.

Police carry the body of Albert Anastasia from the barbershop of New York's Park Sheraton Hotel.

Frank Costello laughs off a bungled attempt on his life. The blood on his lapel attests to the assassin's deadly intent.

Big Paul Castellano in 1959.

Allen Dorfman testifies before a Senate committee in 1957.

Allen Dorfman's body is carried from the parking lot in which one bullet to the head ended his association with organized crime.

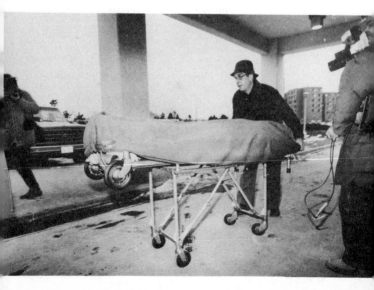

"Crazy" Joe Gallo.

The table in the foreground is the one at which Crazy Joe Gallo ate his last meal. Minutes after he sat down, two gunmen shot him.

Jimmy Hoffa talks with the press in 1974.

One year later, Michigan State Police dig up a field looking for Hoffa's body.

Meyer Lansky.

Joe Colombo lies mortally wounded seconds after his shooting.

Police look over Paul Castellano's body.

Carmine Galante lies dead.

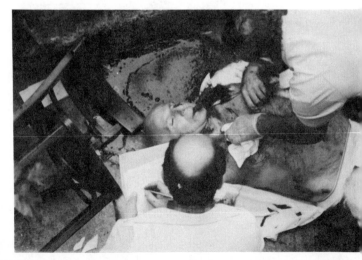

Chapter 11
The Fatal Haircut:
Albert Anastasia

Sometimes the irony in life equals
anything contrived in art....

UMBERTO Anastasio, aka Albert Anastasia, was the
chief enforcer for national organized crime, head of
what had been dubbed Murder, Inc. He was rubbed out
on Friday, October 25, 1957, one month after his fifty-
fifth birthday.

Considering his line of work, he was an old-timer.
He had figured to die in bed and always took precau-
tions to hedge that bet. After forty years of rough work,
even his peers were a little afraid of him. He was the
ogre, the angel of death, dark, brooding, implacable.
Many said they felt a chill in his presence, because he
wasn't just hard on the surface but was ice to the bone.
If you were marked for death by the organization, *he*
became the shadow of doom that would sooner or later
fall over you. It was no wonder he had few intimates.
He had assassinated or planned the assassination of
hundreds of people.

Albert had original ideas for committing murder. In
1935 he wanted to kill a politician, Manhattan Special

Prosecutor Thomas Dewey. Anastasia wanted to get a
baby and a carriage and have someone walk up and
down the street where Dewey lived, pushing the carriage. In it, along with a real baby, there would be a
machine gun equipped with a silencer. When the opportunity presented itself, the gunman pushing the carriage
would open fire and kill the prosecutor. Mob boss Louis
Lepke turned down the scheme, and Dewey went on
to have a long and successful political career. Albert,
needless to say, was upset.

Umberto Aanstasio was born in 1902 in the fishing
village of Tropea on the southern tip of Italy. He was
one of nine sons and three daughters. In 1919 he
arrived in the United States illegally as a seaman. Many
of his brothers had come to this country before him in
the same way.

He adopted the name Albert in 1921 and changed his
last name to Anastasia after his first arrest. He was
busted for murdering another longshoreman. Convicted
of the killing along with a co-conspirator, Albert wound
up in Sing Sing Prison's death row in upstate New
York. For eighteen months he smoked cigarettes, paced
the floor of his cell, and waited to be put to death.
However, his attorney won a new trial for him, at
which he was acquitted. It seems that all the witnesses
who had testified against him in the first trial had
disappeared.

The state freed Albert in April of 1922, unleashing
one of the most feared men in United States crime
history. When young and a little careless, Anastasia
had been arrested five times for various killings, but
the net of justice had wide meshes, and he'd slipped
through each time. Many Mafia buffs felt he'd actually
honored Joe ''The Boss'' Masseria by doing the work

himself when that New York Don was murdered to make way for the crowning of Charlie "Lucky" Luciano as *capo*.

Between 1921 and 1954, Albert was arrested at least ten times, and faced at least five murder raps. He beat all five. Along with his brothers, Albert was linked to extortion, wildcat strikes, assaults, and various murders that occurred along the New York waterfront. Authorities also linked him to rackets involving the garment, laundry, and trucking industries. He dabbled in gambling, too.

However, Albert became best known as the notorious head of a feared society of assassins—Murder, Inc.— which authorities credited with pulling off at least sixty-three killings in New York between 1934 and 1941. There were hundreds more carried out in various cities around the country. What New York cops knew about "The Executioner" was only the tip of the iceberg.

By the 1950s, Anastasia was strong in the garbage business and was virtually lord of narcotics in the United States after his friend Luciano was deported. He had come a long way, he might have reflected with satisfaction, that clear, chilly autumn morning as he left his New Jersey mansion overlooking the Hudson River to begin his last trip to Manhattan. Al wasn't too social at home. His grounds were cordoned off by a ten-foot steel mesh fence with barbed wire at the top. The massive iron gates were kept locked, and two killer dogs roamed the lawns.

That day, he rode in his blue Oldsmobile through the streets of Fort Lee, heading for the George Washington Bridge. He arrived in Manhattan and walked into the Park Sheraton barbershop at approximately 10 A.M.

There were five barbers working that day, plus a manicurist and shoeshine boys. Anastasia waited for his favorite man, so he didn't actually settle into Chair No. 4 until almost 10:30. The owner came and chatted while the barber readied Albert's chair. There were only two other customers now. It was a quiet morning.

Witnesses later said Big Al looked relaxed and satisfied as the striped cloth was adjusted over his body. He closed his eyes and came to a decision: The hot towel would feel just fine on his face. Why not? A shave, haircut, manicure . . .

"Gimme the works," he said.

Just then, two men wearing masks and carrying pistols walked in. They fired ten shots, five of which struck Anastasia in the left hand and wrist. One shot ripped through his hip. When the bullets began hitting him, Anastasia stumbled out of the barber chair. One of the shots struck him squarely in the back.

He crashed into the wall of mirrors in front of him, and a fifth bullet tore into the back of his skull. As the gunmen fled, the people still in the shop ran out in all directions, screaming. The ensuing confusion allowed the shooters to escape almost without notice. The masked men tossed their pistols into the street. One gun was found in the lobby just outside the barbershop; the other was found in a garbage can on Fifty-Seventh Street.

Confusion and bedlam ensued as nearly one hundred detectives converged on the scene while crowds gathered outside. James Leggett, Chief of Detectives at the time, said there were no real leads, so he issued a thirteen-state alarm for the killers. Since Leggett had also led the investigation of the Frank Costello shooting a year before, he knew that the chances of catching

Anastasia's killers were less than slim. Witnesses at the scene described the gunmen as being thirty to forty years old, of average height and build, and wearing fedora hats. That wasn't much to go on in a city of several million. Besides, those descriptions covered half the tough guys in New York at the time. Everybody wore a fedora hat—it was part of a hood's uniform.

At the crime scene, detectives and uniformed cops quickly surrounded the barbers, hotel workers, and passersby who had seen the gunmen flee. The Park Sheraton had been the site of another rubout a few years earlier. In the fall of 1928, gambler Arnold Rothstein was killed in Room 349, presumably for refusing to pay a gambling debt. No one was ever caught in the Rothstein killing, either.

Anastasia's murder came as no surprise. The *New York Times* wasn't playing loose with the facts when they called him "The Executioner." That was his handle on the street. A lot of people might have been gunning for Albert Anastasia, and the killers most likely had strong mob connections, because Anastasia's victims had chiefly been mob members.

Police pieced together the following details of events leading up to his assassination. On the morning of the killing, Anastasia, when he arrived in Manhattan, met with Anthony "Cappy" Coppola, a fat little fifty-year-old gambler, part-time driver, and bodyguard, who lived near Anastasia in Fairview and who sometimes worked in his family's fish business. Coppola looked easygoing but wasn't. He had a bad heart, a bad stomach, and a disposition to match—which may have endeared him to his boss. It was Cappy who was to say of Anastasia after the rubout: "There was one grand guy! Lots of people will cry now that he's dead." As it turned out, Cappy, despite the rhyme in the scan of his statements, was no Mark Antony, and no widespread mourning followed his evocations.

The trouble with rubouts is that most of the time there's no direct confession or testimony, even in the unlikely event someone is charged and brought to trial. The family "hitter" is a tight-mouthed individual from a generally (so far as the law is concerned) uncooperative ethnic background. The reasons for this habit of silence and distrust of authority are not all bad, and have been well-documented elsewhere. For instance, the scene in *The Godfather* where Don Corleone mocks and chastizes the undertaker who was betrayed by the justice system he foolishly trusted makes the general attitude clear.

The details of most rubouts from the killers' point of view have to be deduced and pieced together from secondary evidence such as tapped phone conversations, off-the-cuff remarks made by fringe wiseguys, improper or inadmissable testimony taken in police stations from those trying to take the heat off themselves, emotional outbursts by family and friends of the victims during the first shock following the bad news, and so on. Everyone "knows," for example, that Vinnie "The Chin" Gigante shot Frank Costello in his lobby on Central Park West in the spring of 1957. The "hulking defendant," as the *Daily News* put it, was hauled into court to face the reluctant Costello, who, on the stand, looked blandly at his assailant when asked if he'd happened to notice who'd shot him and said: "I seen no one." It was between them, it was mob business and had nothing to do with the law. In his testimony, there's no sign of fear; it simply becomes clear that

Costello is offended by the State's attempt to punish the man who tried to kill him. So, in Anastasia's case, as in most other gangland slayings, the first question is always: *Cui bono?* Who benefits?

"Cappy" Copolla had no notion. "I didn't think Mr. Anastasia had an enemy in the world," he said.

The New York police had other ideas. Detective Leggett said there were at least 150 angles to this case. The cops watching the funeral had a quiet post. Anastasia was buried in Greenwood Cemetery in Brooklyn after a few prayers from a funeral director in the presence of maybe a dozen mobsters and at least as many detectives.

The first theory in the Anastasia rubout involved the idea that Albert had orderd Frank Costello hit for trying to cut in on his gambling setups. Investigation showed that to be absurd: Costello wasn't a war-oriented *capo,* and the last man on earth to bother, even if he was, would have been Anastasia. A better idea was that Costello was marked for planning to loan Anastasia a couple of million dollars so that he could cut into the then hot pre-Castro Cuban interests. After having bungled the murder attempt on Costello (and alerting him), the only way to block the deal would be to blast Al. A single operator was considered enough for hitting Frank, whereas cutting down Big Al called for a team.

Costello was questioned, naturally, but had no comment. Cappy Coppola went to police headquarters with a lawyer and told his tale. One cop later commented that Cappy could say "I don't know nothin" in nineteen languages. At first, he said he'd been home all day when Al was knocked off; then he remembered he had been to Manhattan to pick up the car his boss had left there—but somehow the car got forgotten downtown where the police later found it. Later still, it came to Cappy that he had, in fact, been supposed to meet Anastasia in the fateful barbershop, but didn't get there until half an hour after the shooting.

While the police didn't stay up nights over the death of Black Albert, at least one law enforcement officer in the city was sorry to see him go. The Bronx District Attorney's office had long wanted to question Anastasia about the murder of Vincenzo Macri in the spring of 1952. Macri, who lived in the Bronx, had been found full of bullet holes, his body stuffed in the trunk of a car. The Bronx DA also wanted to talk to "The Executioner" in connection with the disappearance of Benedetto Macri, Vincenzo's brother. Ten days after Vincenzo's body was found, Bendetto's bloodstained car was found abandoned in Harrison, New Jersey.

So, who killed Albert Anastasia? If anyone knows, he isn't talking. Years after the rubout, a singing bird named Valachi told whoever wanted to listen that Anastasia had become too powerful and had to be eliminated by Vito Genovese to protect himself from revenge by Frank Costello. No one was ever convicted of the crime where "Death finally took The Executioner."

Chapter 12
Rubout by Time: Carlo Gambino

The exception to prove the rule is real!
Carlo Gambino died, untouched,
of old age....

LATE in life, Mafia Don Carlo Gambino tended his prized tomato plants at his modest Long Island home as tenderly as Marlon Brando did in the film, *The Godfather*. Gambino was also known to take leisurely walks in old Italian neighborhoods in the city, chatting quietly with the owners of fruit stands or neighborhood old-timers who recognized him in the street.

It is commonly believed that Gambino was one model for the fictious Don Corleone. Whether Gambino ever was the so-called "Boss of All Bosses" (assuming there ever was such a position) is debatable, but he was, in fact, the head of New York's single most powerful crime family. Gambino, a youthful companion of Lucky Luciano and Meyer Lansky, rose to become Albert Anastasia's second-in-command in the 1940s and 1950s. By careful alliances and selective killings, he eventually became the major force in the five families.

He died quietly of natural causes in his Long Island

home at the age of seventy-four. He had often been described as "courtly," in manners, and outwardly appeared to be a quiet, soft-spoken man. In fact, it was said that nothing in his looks revealed the immense power he wielded in U.S. crime. With his beaked nose and sly smile, he looked like a benign old man.

Mobsters and law enforcers, however, knew another side of this kindly old man. They knew him as a mighty mob boss who presided over the most powerful Mafia crime family in America. He sat on an influential crime commission that called the shots for twenty-six other mob families operating throughout America.

Gambino presided over a thousand or more gangsters, although authorities could never establish precisely how many soldiers he had under his command. With Gambino heading all operations, the family had gambling, labor racketeering, loan-sharking, hijacking, and narcotics interests from western Massachusetts to as far south as Philadelphia. He controlled longshoreman's unions throughout New York City. Unlike many mobsters in the late 1960s and 1970s, Gambino opted to maintain an old-world profile as a low-key power figure. He still lived in a small apartment in Brooklyn when he died, and maintained a modest home on the waterfront in Massapequa, Long Island. His lifestyle, despite his power and widespread influence, reflected his modest beginning in Palermo, Sicily, where he was born in the fall of 1902. His facility as a mob leader also stemmed from those beginnings. He was born in a section of Palermo that had always been tightly controlled by Mafia figures.

Stowing away aboard a ship bound for the United States, Gambino arrived in Newport, Virginia in 1921 and made his way north, settling in Brooklyn down on

Navy Street. Several family members had already settled in New York and were members of Joe "The
Boss" Masseria's crime family. When Masseria was
hit, Gambino moved up in the ranks.

Joseph Valachi, a low-level soldier in the organization, made a name for himself by snitching after he
learned that a contract had been put out for him by
Vito Genovese, once his cellmate at the federal peni-
tentary in Atlanta. Valachi fingered Gambino as the
man who ordered the execution of Anastasia. "He
didn't order it without permission from the Commission," Valachi told investigators. "He had the full sup-
port of the other Mafia bosses." One of those bosses
was Genovese, and "without Vito backing him, Carlo
never would have went for it," Valachi said.

After Anastasia got it, Gambino moved to take over
the crime family, but the move was not without opposition. Aniello Dellacroce, a longtime associate of Anastasia's, protested. A short time later, Gambino
summoned Dellacroce. They declared peace, and Gambino became the undisputed boss of the Anastasia factions in the mob. Gambino's promotion was aimed at
control and power, not money, according to Valachi.

"Him (Gambino) and his brother Paul . . . made
over a million from ration stamps during the war,"
Valachi was quoted as saying in a newspaper account
detailing his testimony in 1962 before a Senate investigating committee. "First, Carlo's boys would steal
them. Then, when the government started hiding them
in banks, Carlo made contact and (government) men
sold him the stamps. He really got rich on that,"
Valachi testified.

Valachi said that Gambino was one of five Mafia
leaders who controlled the New York underworld. The

others were Vito Genovese, Joseph Magliocco, Joseph Bonanno, and Thomas Luchese. Valachi, who said he was committing the worst sin among mobsters by talking, said he decided to come forward after Genovese put out the $100,000 contract on his life because the bosses had been "very bad to their underlings."

The government had been investigating his activities for decades, but it wasn't until 1970 that it appeared they might finally have a case against Carlo Gambino. In that year, the Supreme Court upheld a deportation order against him, based on his illegal entry into the United States, that had been pending since the late 1960s. The high court let stand a lower ruling ordering Gambino deported. These proceedings were started against him by the Immigration and Naturalization Service in 1953. They were stalled repeatedly when Gambino used his medical condition as an excuse not to appear at hearings. Meanwhile, Gambino continued his march to the top of the heap in gangland circles. Authorities in Queens, New York, had been trying to bring Don Carlo before a grand jury investigating the rackets in the borough, but Gambino repeatedly refused to appear, again citing his poor health.

In that instance, Gambino was one of thirteen reputed mob figures arrested as material witnesses for the grand jury while they lunched at La Stella Restaurant in Forest Hills, New York. They were later freed on $100,000 bail each. That grand jury was probing conspiracies in connection with various murders, larceny, and misappropriating of union funds. Interestingly, the American Civil Liberties Union rose to the defense of these men, saying their arrests had been a violation of their civil rights. Like many of the witnesses, Gambino posted bail, but he steadfastly refused to appear before the panel.

The case became a public spectacle when Gambino and the others refused to talk. Queens District Attorney Thomas Mackell was forced to announce his decision to "start from scratch." The same day, the other defendants had appeared in court wearing their best suits, ties, and fedoras. Gambino's attorneys said he was ill and could not appear. The whole thing was dropped when attorneys representing the defendants challenged the legality of their being held as material witnesses on such high bail.

In March of 1970, it appeared the government could finally move against the aging don. In a page-one story, showing the ailing, sixty-seven-year-old Gambino in handcuffs, newspaper accounts said that the "Boss of All Bosses" had been arrested and charged with conspiracy to hijack an armored car. The armored car belonged to Chase Manhattan Bank and contained between three and five million dollars in cash. Federal agents swooped down on Gambino as he rode with his wife and daughter-in-law along Fourteenth Avenue in Brooklyn. An angry Gambino spoke briefly to reporters who converged on the Brooklyn precinct where he was being held. "I'll stay in jail," he said in his soft spoken manner. "I am innocent from this accusation and I won't put up five cents for bail."

Twenty minutes later, however, he allowed a local bail bondsman to post his bail and he went home. Throughout the ordeal, the *Times* said, the frail mobster popped a "heart stimulant pill."

The hold-up never happened; federal agents claimed it was planned by Gambino but the deal went sour when a key figure in the heist rolled over on the conspirators.

It was reported that the plot, hatched the year before, fell through because John J. (Red) Kelley, a bank robber who was brought from Boston to supervise the job, turned informer. Kelley would have been the government's principle witness against the alleged conspirators. Kelley was arrested in May 1969 for the robbery of a Brinks armored truck in Boston. Gambino was to have provided automobiles for the hijacking in New York, and was to have arranged the disposal of the proceeds, while Kelley was to bring down experienced robbers from the Boston "Irish Mob" to do the job.

Appearing before a federal hearing commissioner, Gambino managed to flash a broad smile as he was arraigned before Federal Commissioner Earle N. Bishopp (CQO). Bishopp said that Kelley had proven to be a reliable witness, then ordered Gambino held on $75,000 bond.

In order to avoid testifying, Gambino had his lawyers solicit a battery of doctors who swore that he had a failing heart. In an attempt to refute these medical men, the government ordered an examination by their own doctors. The plan backfired when government-appointed doctors said that Gambino's condition was genuine. He had suffered at least one heart attack, and his condition was described as fragile.

The Feds were certain they had an airtight case against Gambino. The papers, at the time, believed that great strides were being made to stop organized crime. However, Carlo Gambino never spent another minute behind bars, despite vigorous attempts by authorities to put him there.

Gambino died quietly at home. He was buried in a $7,000 bronze casket at a Brooklyn funeral attended by hundreds who came to pay their last respects to one of America's most famous dons.

In his obituary, the *New York Times* said "Mr. Gambino's pre-eimence in crime followed a long succession of violent deaths of other crime figures . . ."

He was buried in a family crypt in Queens amidst wild speculation over who would succeed him. Gambino had avoided the occupational hazards of mob life, and had also successfully eluded authorities. His career had spanned over fifty years. While he was known and feared as one of the most powerful men in crime circles, nobody ever laid a glove on Carlo Gambino.

Chapter 13
Heavy Lunch: Carmine Galante

a classic, with all the trimmings, this
hit ranks with the taking out of
Joe "The Boss" Masseria
at four stars!

STANDING just five feet, four inches tall, he hardly fit
the description of an underworld boss. At the age of
fifty-seven, rotund and balding Carmine Galante could
have been easily mistaken for the corner grocer or even
a wealthy midtown executive if you saw him during his
daily morning jog along the East River, or smoking a
short, black cigar as he rode to work in his chauffeured
car.

This is hardly the image of a man police said was
the kingpin of a crime syndicate. His chauffeur most
likely doubled as his bodyguard, and according to
police, the work he did wouldn't be found among the
government's labor statistics unless murder, narcotics
trafficking, prostitution, pornography, loan-sharking,
and labor racketeering became categories.

Galante had poor eyesight and walked with a slight
stoop, which made him look like a retired grandfather,

not the Godfather he was portrayed to be in thick police dossirs. Those dossiers listed crimes dating back to when Galante was ten years old, growing up in East Harlem, where he was born in 1910.

The son of emigres from the fishing village of Castellammare del Golfo in Sicily, a town famed for the Vendetta, Carmine was labeled incorrigible by authorities at the age of ten and sent to reform school. He landed in Sing Sing at the age of seventeen on an assault charge, and later led a gang of toughs who terrorized the Lower East Side in the 1940s. But the first note of real infamy for "Cigar," as he was known, came in 1943. Police said it was put out on the street that Cigar had a direct hand in the death of Carlo Tresca, editor of a New York anarchist newspaper. The hit was supposedly ordered by Vito Genovese, as a favor to Italy's Fascist leader Benito Mussolini.

Galante's movements were carefully recorded by city, state, and federal authorities. He was married to Helen Galante, the mother of three of his five children. His file listed his chief address as 100 Waverly Place in Greenwich Village. A doorman in the building, however, said he'd never met Galante, or even seen him, for that matter. In fact, he said the only glimpses he ever got of the building's most notorious resident were in the pages of the *Post,* the *Daily News,* or the *Times.*

Galante was a media figure and enjoyed the kind of exposure that unnerves other gangsters who prefer a more anonymous lifestyle. While he remained married to Helen, his dossier revealed a closer liaison with a woman with whom police said the mobster lived for at least twenty years in an apartment on East Thirty-Eighth Street. In fact, they had two children, although the woman was legally married to a friend of Galante's.

The marriage was engineered so that the two children would not be illegitimate.

In the neighborhoods where he was known—chiefly the Bushwick section of Brooklyn, and Manhattan's Lower East Side and Greenwich Village, Galante behaved as if he were an aristocrat, not a mobster. He strolled the streets of the Lower East Side, greeted by locals who sometimes bowed or touched his shoulders lightly as if he were a visiting dignitary or politician. Wherever he went, he could usually be seen smoking a stogie, the trademark that first gave him the nickname of "Cigar" and would later symbolize his violent shooting death. During these downtown walks, he would pick up fruit or vegetables at Balducci's, or stop at DeRoberti's Pastry Shop for cannoli and a cup of espresso. Surveillance teams even photographed him during an uncharacteristic visit to Disney World in Florida. "He was a mass of contradictions," said William Tendy, a former assistant U.S. Attorney who prosecuted Galante in the early 1960s.

Behind this facade, however, was the unchallenged Godfather of the second most powerful crime family in New York. Galante took control of the Joe "Bananas" Bonnano gang after Joe himself was deposed in the 1970s and forced to retire quietly in Arizona. In 1979, with just 200 members in his own family, Galante wanted to oversee all of New York's organized crime families.

While Galante's family was small by mob standards, it was considered one of the most active. Its influence reached from New York to California, from Florida to Arizona.

Galante even dispatched lieutenants to Canada, where he wielded considerable influence over organized crime activities. Nevertheless, authorities considered the Galante family the fourth largest in New York, with the largest being the one-thousand member Gambino family. Authorities credited Galante with controlling most of the heroin shipments from Toronto into the U.S.

In March of 1979, Cigar was freed on $50,000 bail, until a parole hearing could be held, after serving twelve years for the narcotics trafficking charge, and an additional seventeen months for an earlier parole violation. As he emerged from prison, authorities speculate that contract gunmen were ordered to kill Galante by other organized crime families' chieftains. The Queens District Attorney's office believed the execution had been ordered by Frank Tieri, the new head of the crime family started by the late Vito Genovese. A member of the Justice Department's Organized Crime Task Force said that it was Galante's notoriety that incensed other underworld figures and made them want to blow him away. "Crime people resented him because he became a media event and generated too much heat on everyone," said Thomas Puccio, head of the unit in Brooklyn. In an interview in the New York Times in 1979, Puccio said Galante was just blowing smoke when he boasted of succeeding Carlo Gambino as the second "Boss of All Bosses" in United States history.

"I don't think he had any real chance of taking over," Puccio told the papers. "He was wedded to the old system, loan-sharking, gambling, narcotics. That's too risky today for the mob," he said. "He was out of tune with the cleaner, white collar rackets that the mob now prefers."

Through his association with the Bonannos, Galante helped oversee truck hijackings, extortion, and bank-

ruptcy frauds in addition to drugs, gambling and labor
racketeering. The family also ran apparently legitimate
businesses like a cheese company, a garbage carting
service, a clothing business, a jewelry company, and a
trucking company. Galante himself owned a dry clean-
ing business, named L & T Cleaners, on Elizabeth
Street in the Little Italy section of lower Manhattan.
But narcotics remained Galante's special interest.

Galante eventually paid for his ambition to become
a kingpin in the drug trade. In 1960 he was indicted
on drug trafficking charges by a federal grand jury. The
case, however, ended in a mistrial after the foreman of
his jury suffered a broken back following a mysterious
fall. Authorities said the foreman was attacked by
Galante henchmen and brutally beaten. The trial was
interrupted and that jury disbanded.

Two years later, however, Galante was again
indicted on federal narcotics charges, and this time he
was convicted. He was sentenced to twelve years. It
was during this prison stint (he served all twelve years
plus extra time for a parole violation) that he seriously
began to plan to gain sweeping control of all the New
York crime families. From his cell in upstate New
York, he regularly boasted of his plans to associates,
according to police informants and intelligence files.

Examined by doctors while still in prison, Galante
was diagnosed as a psychopath who could not tolerate
being humiliated or losing arguments. Even in prison,
guards gave this squat, chubby mobster a wide berth,
and fellow prisoners knew better than to treat him like
any other con.

LISA Santiago lived in an apartment overlooking a ten-
by-twenty-foot patio behind the Joe and Mary Italian-

American Restaurant at 205 Knickerbocker Avenue in the Bushwick section of Brooklyn. The restaurant was owned by Galante's cousin, Giuseppe Turano. The neighborhood was originally inhabited by German immigrants, and many still lived there in 1979. However, large numbers of Italians immigrated to New York and settled in the Bushwick section between World War I and World War II, many of them coming from Sicily. An earthquake in 1967 brought more Sicilians there. By the late 1970s, Puerto Ricans, blacks, Greeks, Filipinos, Uruguayans, Ecuadoreans, and Chileans had also settled there. Lisa Santiago was among them.

On July 13, 1979, Galante arrived at the restaurant, driven by his nephew, James Galante. The front windows were adorned with simple yellow curtains. The tables were covered with yellow oilcloths with a flowery pattern printed on them. Just inside the door was a picture of the Last Supper. It should have been the "Last Lunch." On another wall was a faded signed photograph of Fernando Lamas. A record album cover with a picture of Frank Sinatra sat on the counter. It was 12:45 and Galante was there for a farewell party for the restaurant's owner, Giuseppe, who was planning to leave the following day for Italy.

Caesar Bonventre and Baldo Amato, associates of Galante followed him into the restaurant and sat down at a table. Leonardo Coppolla, another associate, joined them. Gisueppe invited the three men to join him and Galante on the patio beneath Lisa Santiago's window. They ate lettuce and tomato salad, some rolls were served, and a carafe of red wine was placed on the table. Meanwhile as the three diners quietly ate their afternoon meals, events began to unfold so rapidly that they could only later be pieced together by police from conflicting eyewitness accounts.

At 2:50 P.M., two men in a black Cadillac limousine blocked off traffic on nearby Jefferson Street. At the same time, five other men pulled up in two cars— one gray, the other blue—and parked just outside the restaurant. Three men carrying handguns and shotguns quickly entered, while two others stayed outside and pointed pistols at passersby. Just inside, the three men found young John Turano, Giuseppe's son, a seven-teen-year-old high school student. He was making a phone call.

"Hang up that phone," one of the armed men told the boy. As the kid hung up the men rushed past him toward the rear of the restaurant, ignoring three other patrons who were eating lunch in the second dining room. The men rushed outside onto the patio just as Lisa Santiago was coming down the stairs outside of her apartment facing the restaurant patio.

Less than six feet from Galante's table, the killers opened fire. Bullets and shotgun blasts ripped through Galante's white shirt, which he wore open at the neck. Lisa Santiago stopped dead in her tracks when she heard six shots.

As the bullets tore through his body, Galante clenched his teeth tightly biting down on his cigar. The force of the bullets and shotgun pellets hurled his body backward, and he fell on his back. Blood streaked across his face. Despite the force of the fall, the cigar remained in his mouth even as he lay dead on the patio floor.

Hearing the gunshots, the three unidentified diners inside the restaurant scrambled to the floor. As the gunmen made their way towards the front door, they turned their attention to the witnesses.

A shotgun blast ripped open Coppolla's face. He slumped over and died instantly. A shotgun round hit Giuseppe Turano, blowing off his right shoulder and part of his head. Young John Turano, hearing the shots, raced toward the patio and was shot twice in the back as the gunmen fled past him on their way out. Baldo Amato and Caesar Bonventre, both low-level associates of Galante, were not harmed and fled immediately after the shooting.

A witness overheard one of the killers call one of his companions "Sally" just before they escaped. A neighbor who owned a business two doors down saw the commotion and ran inside to find young John on the floor, bleeding from a gaping bullet wound.

"They got my father," he said, gasping for air, "they got my father."

The noise of so much gunfire drew a crowd outside. The police arrived and found one of the nation's most notorious Mafia bosses dead, still lying on his back with his cigar clenched in his teeth.

Meanwhile, some twenty detectivies fanned out across the city, starting a manhunt for Bonventre and Amato as possible suspects. "We don't know that they set him up," Chief of Detectives James T. Sullivan told *New York Times* reporter Selwyn Raab. "We can't make that assumption at this point." The other obvious possibility was that they went into hiding for fear the gunmen had mistakenly let them escape and would try to finish them off.

As part of their investigation, authorities stepped up their surveillance of organized crime figures throughout the city in an attempt to learn whether they, too, were fearful of becoming victims of what could possibly turn into a gangland war between rival families.

Although police and the FBI made attempts to track down the only solid lead they had—the name Sally— they privately doubted that such a thin lead wold help them find Galante's killers. While investigators had strong suspicions that Galante's death was ordered from high-ranking organized crime figures in the city, they were doubtful of making any arrests in the case. "The O.K. of all of the bosses would have to be involved in the taking of a Godfather," one cop told a reporter. "They're not unhappy by what's happened."

As in life, scandal followed Galante to his grave.

He considered himself a "good Catholic" and a patriot. The Roman Catholic Archdiocese of New York disagreed, refusing to allow a funeral mass to be said for him a week after his assassination.

The church resurrected a little-used statute of ecclesiastical law which prohibited the sacred funeral mass being said for people whose notoriety could possibly cause a scandal. The church offered Galante's family "sympathy," but the office of Terence Cardinal Cooke said, "We are not able to grant a liturgical service in the church because of the scandal that would ensue." Galante was considered a "public sinner" and, as such, did not warrant the same rights as a private sinner.

According to the Canon Law of the Catholic Church, a public sinner is defined as someone "living in public concubinage or in an invalid marriage; those who fail to bring up their children in the Catholic faith; prostitutes, gangsters; those who habitually neglect to make their

'Easter duty' '' of receiving Holy Communion at least once during the Easter season. The *Times* said it marked the first time the New York Catholic Church had refused to hold a funeral mass for a mobster since 1957, after Albert Anastasia's shooting death.

Prayers were said in a small church in Little Italy, while police surveillance teams, reporters, and television camera crews were staked out in front of the Provenzano Lanza Funeral Home on Second Avenue on the Lower East Side. The priest who presided said the Archdiocese allowed him to say only the prayers, not a formal mass. Meanwhile, the church did allow burial masses for both Leonardo Coppolla and his cousin, Giuseppe Turano, because neither were publicly known.

Instead of a church funeral, services for Galante began inside a funeral home, attended by just seventy-five people. Police estimated at least a thousand people watched outside behind police barricades erected to keep dozens of reporters, photographers, and gawkers from disturbing the procession as mourners left for the cemetery in Queens.

As people stepped out of the funeral home into the muggy, hot street, many of them covered their faces, hiding from the frenzy of press activity across the street. Famed lawyer Roy Cohn, who had recently defended Galante in a parole violation hearing, was among them. Galante's wife, Helen, and his mistress both cried during the brief services. Five black limousines waited outside, lined up behind a hearse and three flower cars filled with wreaths. A helicopter carrying a network camera crew buzzed overhead. After a brief graveside service attended by just fifty mourners, the bronze coffin of one of America's most photographed crime bosses was lowered into the ground at St. John's Cemetery. Galante's gang never tried to avenge his murder as far as police authorities knew, and his killers were never found.

Chapter 14
This One Is for You, Frank:
Frank Costello

FRANCESCO Castiglia became famous as Frank Costello, and was often called the "Prime Minister" of the underworld. He was very likely one of the personalities used to create the composite character of Don Vito Corleone in *The Godfather*, representing the surface reasonability of the fictional boss. More than anyone, except perhaps Carlo Gambino (another probable Corleone element) and Chicago's Johnny Torrio, Costello espoused the view that violence was essentially bad for business. The joke had been made, of course, that Frank would only "go to the mattresses"—that is, take cover in preparation for gang warfare—when the stakes were high enough: say, a dollar or more. He was known on the street as just "Frank," as much a superstar in his own world as Elvis or Marilyn or Liz.

Costello was a master bribesman who knew that money, properly applied, could smooth almost any path. It could chop through legal underbrush, make the cops happy they met you, and make a judge a friend for life. While cruder gents settled disputes by blasting away at one another, Frank paid people into submission.

Born in Calabra, Italy, in 1891, his family emigrated to America in 1895. He hailed from the strange, impoverished town of Lauropoli, which, like the United States, was founded in 1776. Lauropoli had a unique constitution: "Anyone who has trouble with justice, or is wanted by the law, is free to come and live in the new town of Lauropoli, where he and his family will have a nice house, work and full protection." Not a bad place for our hero to step onto life's stage, so to speak.

After arriving in the New World, twenty years passed before Frank actually went to jail for anything—he did a short stretch for carrying a pistol. Other than that, there had been only minor arrests for assault and robbery, the first flexing of the youthful muscles of a future crime great, for which he wasn't convicted.

In the 1930s Frank tasted the big time and began cementing powerful relationships with his peers and betters. Some of these relationships would last a lifetime; of course some lifetimes, in his business especially, run a little short.

But among the long-lived were major-leaguers like Charlie "Lucky" Luciano and Meyer Lansky. While Luciano and Lansky stayed busy with the day-to-day work of extortion, racketeering, prostitution, gambling, and eventually, narcotics trafficking, it was the far-seeing Frank who smoothed the way for all these divisions by mastering influence peddling. He was a formidable lobbyist. He delivered votes and raised money for campaigns, etc., until scores of politicians and judges owed him favors. When it came time to make political appointments, Frank Costello was virtually a one-man senate exercising "advise and consent." Between 1920 and 1930 it was alleged that he paid close to $20,000 per week to city and federal officials! When a foolish prosecutor or cop arrested the wrong people, the "right" judge would get assigned to the case and things "would be straightened out."

No one seriously questioned how Frank spent some monies. He was a true mafiosi, in the original sense, a man of honor and power. His results spoke for themselves. His honor, as we've seen, made him one of the few people ever actually jailed for contempt for refusing to identify the man who tried to kill him.

In 1951, before the Senate Crime Investigation Committee, Frank Costello became a television personality. All agreed he handled himself rather coolly. Chairman Estes Kefauver tried his best to unravel the mob's inner workings, but Costello wasn't much help, sitting calmly in a basket-weave blue suit and maroon tie. When the chief counsel for the investigating committee, Rudolph Halley, asked Costello whether or not he had ever used his mother's name, the following Abbott-and-Costello routine ensued:

> Halley: Now what do you mean when you say you *might* have used the name Saverio? Don't you know very well you used the name Saverio?
>
> Costello: I might have used it, yes.
>
> H: I will not accept that answer. Did you or did you not use it?
>
> C: Well, I might have.
>
> H: Well, you know you used it, do you not?
>
> C: Well, I don't know. I won't say I didn't.

H: Well, you are not using the English language
when you say you might have. That means
nothing.

Wolf: (Interjecting) He generally uses the English
language.

C: I'm sorry I am not a college man like you, Mr.
Halley.

H: Thank you very much. But can you tell us
whether you ever used the name of Frank
Saverio?

C: Why should I? Isn't that answer good enough
for you?

Later, Frank was pressed on the high points of his
past career by the nosy senators who, now and then,
incorrectly referred to him as the "defendant" rather
than a witness:

Kefauver: Now, Mr. Costello, bearing in mind
that you are under oath, will you state
whether or not prior to having been nat-
uralized as a citizen of the United
States, you were engaged in the illicit
liquor business in the United States?

Costello: I was not.

K: You were admitted to citizenship, were you
not, on Sept. 10, 1925? Prior to the month of
September, 1925, did you or did you not
engage in the business of selling, purchasing,
transporting or possessing alcoholic beverages
in the United States contrary to law?

C: No.

K: And what did you do and what did you not
do?

C: I didn't sell no liquor prior to 1925, and I had nobody representing me personally in Canada. I might have expressed it the wrong way, that people that went there and bought and come on here and I bought it from them.

K: Was Harry Sausser one of the people that you bought liquor from?

C: There might have been a Sausser or a Harry Sausser.

K: How many Harry Saussers did you know?

C: I don't know—I might have known two or three.

Senator: Do you expect us to believe this tale of the flying Saussers?

C: I am not expecting you to believe anything. I knew you weren't going to believe anything when I first come here. I have been prejudged.

Frank always seemed a little nonplussed by the fact that people were paying him for his services, if you judge by the transcripts:

Halley: Then you had an income in 1949 from George Morton Levy (head of Roosevelt Raceway, president of the Nassau County Bar Association and one-time counsel for Luciano) of $15,000. Would you mind telling the committee again what that was for?

Costello: I met Mr. Levy and Mr. Levy told me that he was having difficulty at the race track, at the Roosevelt Raceway. He thought that he might lose his franchise, his interest. Bookmakers were there, and

the Racing Commmission told him that
if he didn't clean it up, he might jeopar-
dize his license. He asked me to help
him.

I says, "What way can I help you?"
He says, "Can you suggest something?"
I say, "Well, haven't you got a detective agency there?" He says, "I have."
I says, "Well, if they can't help you,
how can I help you?" He says, "Well,
it seems that there's a lot of complaints.
I personally don't think there's any more
bookmakers there than any other track,
but there's a lot of complaints."

I says, "Nothing I can do for you,
George." So he says, "Maybe you can
think of something."

I says, "Well, what can I do, George?
I can spread the propaganda around that
they're hurting you there, and you're a
nice fellow, and I can tell them that if
there's any arrest made it's going to be
very severe. I don't now how much
good it's going to do you, but I'll talk
about it."

He says, "I wish you would." And I
did.

H: Do you think that your passing the word
   around would have such an influence on
   bookmakers?

C: I didn't think so and I still don't think so.

H: Did you think that your services were worth a
   total of $60,000 over four years?

C: Which is $15,000 a year. No, I didn't think
    so.

H: What did you do in 1946 to earn $15,000?

C: Practically nothing.

H: Well, just what did you do, unless it was abso-
    lutely nothing?

C: Outside of just talking about it, that bookmak-
    ers are going to hurt this man's license, and
    they cannot make enough money there to hurt
    a man or to take a chance on account of the
    severe penalty they would get if they got
    arrested.

Senator: Can you give any explanation of what
          further you did or what Mr. Levy said
          you were to do or sought from you infor-
          mation as to what you did?

C: Well, I don't know. I'm under the impression
    there was no such thing as bookmakers there
    of any amount to be frightened.

Frank's services were subtle, in certain respects, and
it was easy to make him seem somewhat absurd, as
the senators did under questioning. After all, selling
influence backed by a powerful and dangerous organization like *La Mafia,* isn't like drawing a paycheck with
a pension plan at the end of it.

Costello ran into more trouble in the 1950s during a
major investigation of Tammany Hall, when his name
came up repeatedly in connection with payoffs, bribes,
and kickbacks. Many major New York political figures
were brought down at that time, including former
Mayor William O'Dwyer, who later became U.S.
ambassdor to Mexico. Many city commissioners took
falls for being on Costello's "pad." In March 1951,

national television carried stories about Costello's background and present status, such as his known real estate holdings, the fact that he owned part of a TV station himself, and was a close business partner with the legendary Meyer Lansky. He was then in trouble for income tax evasion and the Feds were depicting him as an undesirable who ought to be deported back to Italy.

Frank didn't see it that way. He said in the early 1900s he'd worked in a piano factory and dabbled in real estate. Spectators and some of the senators questioning him didn't bother to hide their laughter. Frank stayed cool, saying that he later became involved in the manufacture of Kewpie dolls, plastic toys that one senator alleged were used as prizes in an illegal gambling operation.

Frank remained unflappable. It is worth noting, in this regard, that his eventual next-door neighbor-but-one in the semi-exclusive Sands point district of Long Island was Roy Cohn—which is probably a form of karma or, at least, synchronicity.

When asked, to trap him into endangering his U.S. citizenship, if he'd been a bootlegger in the early 1920s, he responded, "I didn't get involved with booze until 1925. That was after I became an American."

The various investigations finally trapped him into a tax battle with the IRS, and he eventually did face deportation. It took the government nearly eight years to get the goods on him, but by 1957 wily Frank was out on bail pending an appeal of his tax convictions. Unfortunately for him, he had worse problems by then—Don Vito Genovese was about to strike. As a young Mafia associate once put it: "These wiseguys (meaning 'made' men) don't have it easy. You got the cops and the feds on one side. You got the bandits freelancing to rip you off. And you got your friends to worry about too, the second you slip up or let up."

There was a story circulating that Don Vito wanted to block a Costello/Anastasia move in Cuba—then wide open under Batista, a mobster himself in most respects—and chew up a chunk for himself. So he made the deal tough by clipping Albert in the famous barber chair, at the same time sending a second pincer movement to take out long-suffering and (hopefully) distracted Frank Costello. Our Frank was hard to lick because, on the whole, he didn't know the meaning of the word impossible. To judge from the transcript, he didn't know the meanings of many other words either, as Gilbert Choate said in an article.

Either Costello's luck held or Genovese had a surprise sense of humor, because he supposedly sent Vinnie "The Chin" Gigante alone to take out Frank. On May 2, 1957, the police speculated that Gigante headed north to Central Park West to await Costello. After his target arrived at No. 214, the hulking Vinnie lumbered into the hallway after him, brushed aside the doorman, and called out the immortal words: "This one is for you, Frank!" With that Vinny drilled one "upside" Frank's head. Apparently Vinny saw Costello's hat fly off and blood run and was satisfied. He had no desire to make sure. There's almost a sense that he felt badly about the whole thing at the last minute—hitmen aren't usually that careless—but business is business. In this case it was no sale, and Don Frank lived to be harassed by the authorities yet again.

Gigante had been identified by the doorman (though he'd lost forty pounds and cut his hair off) and was on trial for the botched hit. They confronted Frank with his hat. It was evident that the bullet had gone in the front and exited the rear. The prosecuting attorney put it on. He didn't care what the experts said, he declared, he had been shot from behind. He swore he'd never laid eyes on "Chin" before.

C. I don't know of any human being who would have a notion to want to kill me.

PA: Isn't it a fact that you know who shot you?

C: Absolutely not!

PA: Over the years you had a lot of disagreements with people in the underworld—isn't that a fact?

C: No, it's not a fact.

PA: I'll ask you for the last time to tell the truth. Who shot you?

C: Well, I'll ask you. Who shot me?

PA: I'm asking you!

C: I don't know!

PA: And you saw no one?

C: I seen no one.

The upshot was that Frank went to Atlanta and while in the pen made "the peace" with Don Vito. Upon his release he retired from active service. No one shot at him again.

He can almost be remembered as a peacemaker in an odd setting who once told Charlie Luciano: "Violence is ignorance." All things considered, he was a remarkable individual.

Chapter 15
Upsetting the Applecart:
Frank Scalise
A Hitter Hit

IT began as just a stroll to pick up some fruit and vegetables at a greengrocer's store in the heavily populated Crotona-Fordham section of the Bronx. It ended when two gunmen pumped at least three bullets into fifty-five-year-old Frank Scalise, an underworld crime figure closely associated with crime boss Frank Costello.

The assassination was carried out on an afternoon in June 1957, effectively eliminating one of the most powerful gang leaders in New York history. Scalise had just walked out of a market on Arthur Avenue when he was sighted by the killers, who fired five shots, hitting him three times. They fled to a black sedan waiting double-parked in front of the store, leaving one of the kingpins of a major international drug-smuggling ring, and the heir-apparent to Mafia leadership on the ground. Scalise's murder came closely on the heels of a similar attempt on Frank Costello, a known mobster who nearly got it a few weeks earlier in the lobby of his apartment building at 214 Central Park West. Authorities said Costello had close ties to Charles "Lucky" Luciano, a Mafia overlord who had recently been deported. Luciano and Scalise were also business partners, police said.

According to press reports at the time of his murder, Scalise owned stock in the Mario & DiBono Plastering Company in Corona, Queens. His real business was smuggling narcotics through international connections. Why he was killed was open to speculation.

"He was regarded as a big shot and a kingpin," said Bronx District Attorney Daniel Sullivan. "Thus far, this appears to be definitely a gangland killing."

For over a year, the police had wanted to discuss with Scalise the murder of Vinnie Macri, and the mysterious disappearance of Macri's brother, Benedetto. Vinnie's body had been found in the trunk of a car in the Bronx in the spring of 1954. He had been shot twice in the head at close range. Police later found bloodstains in a car which had been used by Benedetto, which suggested, he, too, had been clipped. Both men were considered underworld figures. Bendetto was tried in 1949 for the ice-pick murder of William Lurye, an organizer for the International Ladies Garment Workers Union. However, he was acquitted after a key witness recanted his testimony.

Scalise had been sought by various federal and local authorities for a long list of crimes, including murder and narcotics cases. He was arrested as early as 1920 in connection with burglary and robbery in New Rochelle, New York, but was never convicted. In 1953 he was the target of an investigation into the murder of a man in a Bronx restaurant, and also for the murder of Dominick Calicci, killed in a Bronx shooting the same year. Two years later, in June of 1955, police wanted Scalise to testify before a Senate committee investigating narcotics trafficking. However, lawyers stalled his appearance, saying he was recovering from an operation.

Shortly after Scalise was gunned down, authorities descended on his home on City Island in the Bronx and confiscated boxes of records, address books and other documents. His 1956 Cadillac was impounded for possible evidence. In the car they found an address book and a wallet. At his house they impounded a huge leather case and boxes of photographs and other miscellaneous papers. Acting on a tip, five men were hauled downtown for questioning but were later released.

At his funeral less than a week later, federal agents used a surveillance technique that later became routine. Plainclothes cops photographed the coming and going of mourners both at the funeral home and later at nearby Woodlawn Cemetery. As more than twenty cars were loaded with mourners, they photographed as many individuals as possible for later identification. Later, the agents subpoenaed the records of all visitors, including anyone who sent flowers or sympathy cards to the family of the slain mobster. Pressing the power of subpoena further, the government got hold of Scalise's bank records. They discovered that the powerful mob figure had a mere $950 in cash, $2,000 in bonds, and some jewelry belonging to his wife squirreled away in a safe deposit box. Police also found coded personal records in a subsequent search of the Scalise City Island home. The records contained at least one hundred names, many of which were well-known political and civic figures.

The case was brought before a grand jury in April

of 1959. The Bronx grand jury was empaneled to look into what were described as the "peculiar" circumstances surrounding Scalise's brother Gioivanni, who fled the United States a short time after his brother Frank was murdered. In addition, the grand jury was asked to examine the disappearance of another Scalise brother, Joseph, who turned up missing two weeks after the killing. The sixty-year-old Giovanni was picked up early in 1959 in Mexico City as he was about to leave for Rome. The brothers had nothing much to say, except that they'd felt a sudden urge to "see the world."

Chapter 16
Death on the Half Shell:
Joey Gallo

THE shooters who blasted "reformed" mobster "Crazy Joe" Gallo as he ate clams in the early morning hours of April 7, 1972 did not enjoy one of the benefits that had become standard practice in their trade—the code of silence.

Less than a year after gunmen pushed their way into Umberto's Clam House in Little Italy and picked off Crazy Joe, somehow avoiding his new bride and other members of his family, an informer spilled his guts on the witness stand in New York State Supreme Court. In previous mob killings police always speculated publicly about which rival faction might have been responsible. However, it was rare that one of the hitters himself turned state's evidence and testified in open court, naming names.

But in December of 1972, just eight months after Gallo was shot and killed, prosecutors pursuing a weapons charge against a Gallo associate had Joseph Luparelli on the stand implicating members of the Joe

Colombo family in Gallo's death. Luparelli was appearing at the trial of Peter Diapoulas, a longtime friend of Gallo, who was with him the night he was killed at Umberto's. Diapoulas was on trial for illegal possession of a .25-caliber pistol which authorities said he was carrying when Gallo was killed.

Crazy Joe was assassinated as he celebrated his forty-third birthday, a time in his life when he was working hard to change his image. In fact, he had recently announced plans to help bolster the civil rights work of the Americans of Italian Descent and was often seen cavorting with well-known society figures instead of with mobsters. His execution was carried out with swift precision, although Luparelli testified it had not been planned in advance. The hit, he said, was carried out on impulse, when he and other gang members spotted Joe entering Umberto's Clam House on Mulberry Street.

Luparelli, a self-described fence, chauffeur, and bodyguard for Joey Yacovelli, the new head of the Colombo gang, could hardly be heard in parts of the courtroom. Authorities said Yacovelli took control of the Colombo family after a gunman believed to have been hired by Joey Gallo fatally wounded Joe Colombo during a civil rights rally.

"Yacovelli had been Colombo's *consigliere,*" Luparelli said, speaking in a low, hoarse voice. As *consigliere,* Luparelli said, Yacovelli advised the gang on who should be hit and who should not. He was suggesting that Yacovelli had endorsed the killing of Gallo in retaliation for the murder of Colombo by a man allegedly hired by Gallo.

Luparelli showed up on the doorstep of FBI agents less than two weeks after Gallo's murder, willing to confess all if the agents would place him in protective custody. According to press reports at the time, he arrived in court surrounded by at least a dozen plain-clothes detectives and another half dozen uniformed court officers.

"I was standing outside a restaurant downtown owned by Matty Iannello about four-thirty when I see Gallo pull up," Luparelli said.

"This was on the morning of April 7," said Assistant District Attorney Robert Tannenbaum, the prosecuting attorney.

"Right," Luparelli whispered.

"Continue please!"

"I strolled down Mulberry Street and went inside another restaurant where I spoke to Philip Gambino and Carmine 'Sonny' DiBiase, telling them what I just seen," Luparelli said.

"Tell us who these two men are, please," the prosecutor asked.

"Both are Colombo men and we had been talking about getting Crazy Joe for some time now and this was a good opportunity to do it, I thought."

"What happened in the next forty-five minutes?" the prosecutor asked.

"I told them Joey Gallo was down the street. Sonny wanted to know what he was doing. I told him I didn't know but they were starting to eat. Sonny ordered somebody to get some guns," said Luparelli. A few minutes later, he said, four men—Sonny, Gambino, and two brothers known only by the names of Sisco and Benny—drove down Mulberry Street in two cars.

Days after the killing, newspaper accounts of the shooting quoted wild speculation based on police informants as to who might have wanted to kill Crazy Joe.

At the time, Luparelli's involvement was not known. Apparently, a lot of people might have wanted Joey Gallo dead. Although the Colombos were high on most people's lists as the gang most likely to succeed, there was little evidence linking Colombo's people to the killing.

Gallo's death, by conservative estimates, was one of at least twelve killings which occurred between 1960 and 1972 due to a series of gangland wars. According to police files, the wars against Gallo started in the early 1960s and stemmed from his feud with Carmine Persico, a top lieutenant in the Colombo family, when Joey and his brothers, Albert "Kid Blast" and Larry, opposed Joseph Profaci, the family boss. A member of the Vito Genovese family, Tony Strollo, jumped in on the side of the Gallo brothers, hoping to take over some of Profaci's racketeering operations.

Persico and a lieutenant, Joseph Scimone, were indicted that same year for attempting to strangle Larry Gallo, but the charges were later dismissed. Joey Gallo, meanwhile, was charged with conspiracy and extortion in 1961 in connection with an attempt to muscle in on the check-cashing and bar business of Teddy Moss, a Brooklyn businessman. It was his twenty-third arrest and fourth conviction, and the judge vowed in open court that he would put the career criminal away for as long as the law allowed. In his remarks, Judge Joseph A. Saraflte denounced the current war between Gallo and Persico, dumping the blame for a rash of killings and wanton violence squarely on Gallo's shoulders, although he had not been officially charged in any of those incidents.

"Gallo's conviction arose from a brazen and ruthless attempt to muscle in on the business of Mr. Moss," said the DA, Paul Kelly, who was quoted in one newspaper account of the trial. "He showed savage disregard for standards and mores of an orderly society."

Then Kelly cited a litany of shootings, stranglings, kidnappings, and mysterious disappearances and said, "since the defendant was remanded (to police custody), there have been no known offensive actions taken by the Gallos in this dispute. This gives credence to the belief that Joe Gallo is in reality the sparkplug and the enforcer in the mob and his absence from the immediate scene has accounted for the lack of sustained violence on the part of his associates." Kelly was quoted extensively in the *New York Times*, a newspaper which rarely covered routine court stories. But Joey Gallo was a kind of anti-hero, a flamboyant gangster who was a legend in his own time.

Legend or not, Judge Sarafite gave Gallo seven to fourteen years in Sing Sing. Someone tried to poison him while he was waiting to be transferred upstate, but the plot was discovered. At about the same time, Strollo disappeared and never surfaced again. The war continued, even while Gallo was safely locked up miles from the center of things in Manhattan and Brooklyn.

Joey Gallo did eight years and reportedly sent several black inmates whom he had met in the joint back to Brooklyn to contact members of his gang. Meanwhile, Profaci died of natural causes and was replaced by Joseph Magliocco, his brother-in-law.

The war against Gallo associates continued. Magliocco died a short time later, and Joseph Colombo took over the family. It was Colombo who negotiated a successful peace treaty in 1964 with the help of New England Mafia boss Raymond Patriarca. While Joey was in prison, the gang was headed by Larry. When Larry died in 1968, the Gallo influence began to decline, even though Albert Gallo tried to keep things together.

Joey emerged from prison in 1971 and denounced the 1964 treaty as null and void, since he had not personally taken part in the negotiations. Gallo immediately moved to take over the Brooklyn-based rackets operated by the Colombos.

As Colombo lay in critical condition in a Manhattan hospital, after the famous Columbus Day hit, his associates vowed to get Joey Gallo, although there was no real evidence that Colombo's hitman had been hired by the Gallo organization.

DESPITE these activities, Joey Gallo made it widely known that he wanted a new image. He worked hard after his release from jail to cement that idea in the minds of both the public and the new crowd he courted. Joey chose entertainers, writers, and civic causes, and anything else associated with glamorous society. New York *Newsday* columnist Jimmy Breslin wrote a book, *The Gang That Couldn't Shoot Straight,* and many speculated that the book and subsequent movie were about Crazy Joey and his gang.

Trading in his police record for tickets to Broadway shows, Gallo called well-known entertainment figures to chat casually. The *New York Times* said he once called actress Joan Hackett a "broad" and endeared himself to her, too.

Gallo offered his services to a group called the Americans of Italian Descent, a civil rights group and a legitimate lobbying organization. While it appeared to be a genuine gesture, AID, as it was called, had the same goals as the Italian-American Civil Rights League, the group founded by Gallo's arch rival, Joseph A. Colombo, Sr. But organizers of AID, while skeptical of Gallo's motives, decided he was sincere and assigned his men to act as recruitment representatives at the organization's headquarters at 400 Madison Avenue in New York City.

The end came in classic gangland style—bloody and dramatic.

While celebrating his birthday, Gallo had spent the early part of the night drinking champagne at the Copacabana with Sina, her daughter from an earlier marriage, ten-year-old Lisa Essary, and his sister, Mrs. Carmella Fiorello. Also with him was Peter Diapoulas and his date, Edith Russo. Riding in a black Cadillac with bumper stickers advertising the Italian civil rights organization he had joined just the day before, they sped downtown around four o'clock in the morning and cruised slowly down Mulberry street near Umberto's. Gallo had never been to the clam house and was venturing onto unfamiliar turf. Joey was a Brooklyn boy playing in someone else's backyard that night. Nevertheless, they parked the car and were welcomed inside by the owners.

The party was seated at two butcher-block tables in the back of the restaurant. Joey and Diapoulas put their backs to the wall, the others sat facing them. They ordered food later described by police as "Italian delicacies." Luparelli, the federal witness who broke the sacred code of silence, said Sonny DiBiase and the two brothers, Sisco and Benny, walked into Umberto's about forty-five minutes after Luparelli spotted Gallo and his group go inside. Gallo, who was unarmed, had just ordered a second helping, when a lone gunman dressed in a light tweed coat pointed a pistol at him. The shooting started. Women screamed. Customers dove for cover on the floor and behind tables as the gunman emptied his gun, a heavy gauge handgun that was later identified as a .38. Although the police account only describes a single gunman, Luparelli indicated there were probably at least three. Witnesses said that Diapoulas pulled a gun and returned fire. The police later reported that at least four guns and twenty rounds were fired in the brief melee.

Gallo was mortally wounded. He rose and staggered out the front door, his killers still pumping bullets into his now bloody body. The gunmen fled through the rear door, jumped into a waiting car, and escaped.

Gallo staggered toward his car, collapsed, and died on the street. His sister screamed hysterically. Her screams were heard by a passing police patrol, who picked up his body and raced to a hospital, where efforts to revive him failed. Diapoulas had minor wounds and was treated and released.

Luparelli became a snitch only after he suspected his own life was in danger just two weeks after he helped finger Gallo. He said the Colombo boys planned to kill him and his family. Luparelli fled to California and agreed to break the code of silence in return for his safety.

Although he had gone underground, the government named Sonny DiBiase as Gallo's killer. However, they could not indict him for the killing. In fact, even though DiBiase and Gambino were implicated by a co-conspirator, an indictment was impossible on the strength of

Luparelli's testimony without corroborating evidence. As an accomplice, Luparelli himself was never charged. As a witness, his testimony against his pals in the Gallo murder was inadmissable. Gambino was eventually nabbed, but not for the Gallo murders. The best they could do was get him on a parole violation and criminal contempt for refusing to testify before a grand jury in the Gallo case.

THE government subpoenaed dozens of witnesses to appear before a grand jury, a venerable laundry list of underworld figures. One by one, they either refused to testify or were later charged with lying before the grand jury. Assistant District Attorney Robert Tannenbaun said that no one was talking because each feared becoming the next victim.

In fact, the only tangible arrest made in the case was that of Peter Diapoulas, Gallo's friend and associate. Witnesses said he fired at the Gallo killers.

No one was ever convicted of killing Crazy Joey Gallo, even though authorities believed Luparelli's story of what happened that morning on Mulberry Street.

Meanwhile, friends and relatives, cops and government agents gathered at Gallo's wake. Women sobbed painful good-byes. His mother, Mary Gallo, cried, "My Joey, my Joey," as she was helped from the building by relatives. Jerry and Marta Orbach were among the grievers as was the Broadway director of *Oh Calcutta*, Jacques Levy. Scores of reporters and photographers hovered outside the funeral home before the burial.

As family members emerged, some being helped by others, photographers began snapping pictures wildly.

When one of them tried to get a close-up of one of the Gallo women, a man interrupted him by asking, "You're not going to write anything I'm going to get upset about, are you?" The *New York Times* reported.

Chapter 17
There is no Mafia:
Joseph Colombo, Sr.

In keeping with the Civil Rights spirit
of the times, Joe Colombo was
assassinated, but, unlike
Martin Luther King, Jr.,
they have yet to establish a
national holiday in his honor.

THE blood on his face was already hardened and brown
when Joseph A. Colombo, Sr. was wheeled, unconscious, through the emergency room doors of Roosevelt
Hospital. The head of one of New York's most visible
crime families was near death.

It was June 28, 1971. Just minutes before, the forty-
eight-year-old Colombo had been shot twice by a black
gunman. Emergency room doctors moved swiftly that
summer afternoon, desperately trying to pump life back
into his traumatized body. Around him milled dozens
of plainclothes detectives, blood relatives, and certainly
a few armed members of Colombo's crime family.
Some, including Colombo's twenty-six-year-old son
Joseph, Jr., still had his blood on their hands and
clothing.

In an adjacent room lay the dead body of Jerome A.
Johnson, a New Brunswick, New Jersey, man identified

as Colombo's would-be assassin. Who was Johnson, and how was he able to get so close to such a powerful gangleader?

Once a longshoreman, Joseph Colombo, Sr. rose through the ranks of a New York gang. Early in his career he was ordered to assassinate three top Mafia leaders; Carlo Gambino, Thomase Luchese, and Stephano Magddino. He punked out and told Gambino his orders had come from then-powerful New York boss Joe Bonanno. In a rare show of mercy, Bonanno was forced to retire from mob activities. Eventually, Colombo became leader of the Profaci family and was rewarded with a seat on the national crime syndicate.

When he took the seat, he was immediately confronted by the Gallos. Since he had risen to power by neither muscle nor brain power, but by the simple expedient of being regarded as a "fink," his position was always uncertain. Almost immediately after he rose to the rank of syndicate boss, Colombo began his misadventure with the Italian-American Civil Rights League. He publicly ridiculed his portrayal by the media as a mob kingpin, saying sardonically, "There is no Mafia."

The League, started by Colombo in 1970, claimed to have some 45,000 members by June 28, 1971. On that day when Colombo was shot, the League was rallying in Columbus Circle in Manhattan to protest what they described as the constant harassment of Italian-Americans by police and federal authorities, especially the FBI.

According to police sources, however, Colombo was not a typical civil rights activist. They characterized him as the Godfather of a crime family that numbered more than two hundred. His shooting, they said, was significant in a number of ways. First, Jerome Johnson had carried out a professional hit, despite the fact he appeared to be a drifter, unconnected to any mob. Second, police said, the hit marked the first time in at least fourteen years that a major mob figure was the target of a shooting in the city. The last incident had involved mobster Frank Costello, sometimes called the Prime Minister of Crime, and the kingpin of a national crime syndicate.

The details of the successful Colombo hit were less clear. Who had sent Jerome Johnson? Who fired the shots that killed Johnson where he stood seconds after Colombo was shot? These and many other questions related to the shooting remained unanswered as Colombo was moved from the emergency room to be prepared for surgery.

The police knew that any number of people could have ordered the Colombo hit. However, the name that sprang immediately to everyone's mind on both sides of the law was Gallo—Crazy Joey and his brother Albert. The Gallos had a long-standing feud with Colombo that dated back at least ten years.

"The brothers were reputed to head a faction in the Mafia family that the Justice Department has said is under the Colombo's leadership," newspapers reported. "Federal, state and local authorities said there had been increasing friction between the Gallo faction and the parent group." In fact, Gallo had plans to align himself with a rival Italian-American civil rights group.

The trouble was believed to stem from a 1960 feud when the Colombo family was led by Joseph Profaci. According to Joe Valachi, the Gallos, including Larry Gallo (who died in 1968), felt Profaci was chiseling their share of the family's profits, so they struck back by abducting a few of Profaci's family members, holding them in assorted houses and apartments until Profaci loosened his purse strings.

However, the *New York Times* reported that Profaci went back on his word once they were released. A top Gallo lieutenant disappeared a short time later, and someone tried to kill Larry Gallo.

"The gang war that followed resulted in at least twelve killings," the newspaper said. "At the height of the war (in 1961), the Gallos holed up in what came to be known as the Dormitory, the second floor running through two connected brick buildings at 49-51 President Street in Brooklyn."

Profaci died in 1962 and was replaced by Joseph Magliocco, the Profaci brother-in-law kidnapped by the Gallos. When Magliocco died in 1963, *New York Times* reporter Nicholas Gage said that Colombo rose to power and arranged a truce.

The Gallos supposedly agreed to the truce because they were too weak to go on fighting. Larry Gallo was sick and Crazy Joe had gone to jail two years before, leaving only Albert to carry the family torch.

In the spring of 1971, when Joey Gallo was released from jail, the hostilities resumed. Among other things, Joey complained that Colombo had become too visible as leader of the ill-conceived Italian-American Civil Rights League. Other powerful figures, including Carlo Gambino, were less than pleased with Colombo's hunger for publicity. Also, reports had been leaked from Attica State Prison, where Gallo had served time for extortion, that Joey had suffered "cruel and unusual punishment" for his work on behalf of black inmates. When he filed a suit in New York State Supreme Court to that effect, the scuttlebutt coming out of Attica was confirmed. Therefore, had the Gallos recruited Johnson to hit Colombo?

Jerome Johnson was a small-time thief. He had been arrested at least seven times for rape and robbery, but never did any hard time. He had repeatedly been arrested by the campus police at Rutgers University near his home in New Brunswick for hanging out at the dorms without proper ID. A drifter, he spent some time in California and had returned to New Jersey shortly before the shooting. When he returned, he had a clean-shaven head, and told friends he had shaved his hair off "because of the organization." Police said Johnson had dealings with a labor union, and that was the organization he referred to when asked about his appearance.

In short, Johnson was an unlikely assassin for the likes of Joseph Colombo, and an even more unlikely friend of Joey Gallo.

Chief of Detectives Albert Seedman held a news conference the day after the shooting to answer reporter's questions.

"It was the work of one nut, one fanatic," Seedman told newsman. However, this nut seemed to know something about the mechanics of pulling off a professional hit. For one thing, he obtained forged press credentials and was able to get close to Colombo through the press box. He had armed himself with a 7.65-millimeter automatic weapon. When he began shooting, he hit his target at least twice—the mark of a professional hitman, not an aimless drifter.

The cops explored all leads, including Gallo's possible connection. They even questioned Carlo Gambino and other reputed Mafia figures. Colombo's shooting caused a variety of reactions in the underworld. Some feared they'd be blamed for the hit, and many stayed close to their homes under tight security.

"Considering the history of the underworld's plot and counterplot, members would not have been surprised if someone close to Colombo had been involved," said the *New York Times*.

Crime boss Carlo Gambino had openly frowned on so public a hit, and one federal official was quoted as saying, "The boys feel it's not Gambino's style; it's not something he would have wanted."

And yet, one might imagine a conversation as follows among those would benefit from this assassination:

"If we get a black to do the job on Colombo, then they're going to figure it was Crazy Joey, because he's known to have been buddies with niggers in the can."

"Yeah. Then we can get rid of fucking Joey, too."

"In other words, two for the price of one."

LESS than an hour after the shooting, the planned rally for "unity" among Italian-Americans resumed at the foot of a statue of Christopher Columbus, which had been covered with red, white, and green plastic streamers—the colors of the Italian flag.

The Reverend Louis Gigante, chaplain of the League, had just returned from the hospital, where he had given Colombo Last Rites. City officials, including Representative Mario Biaggi and the future mayor, Abe Beame, then controller of the city, spoke to hundreds of people who had gathered for the rally. Mayor John Lindsey called the shooting "an ugly shock to all New Yorkers."

Shortly after 3 P.M. the rally ended.

There had been several incidents directly related to the shooting. A black musician who had volunteered to entertain the crowd found himself at the mercy of their anger after the shooting. The man was beaten and his instruments were taken by angry men in the crowd. Black reporters in the press box were immediately ejected from the area near the podium until white reporters interceded on their behalf and they were allowed to continue covering the rally.

Senator John J. Marchi, a Republican from Staten Island, New York, who had often opposed the Italian-American Civil Rights League, was quick to say that the assassination attempt had been "a numbing and stunning turn of events. It points up again in a very dramatic way that the whole operation was poorly conceived, and I hope that law enforcement agencies are investigating this in all of its ramifications."

WAS Joseph Colombo, Sr. an activist or a mob boss?

Apparently, he was both at the same time, although law enforcement officials believed his role as a civil rights activist was at least a part of the reason why he now lay near death in a Manhattan hospital.

"Mr. Colombo apparently played many roles in his active life," said Brooklyn real estate owner and agent Anthony Canalupo. "For instance, Mr. Colombo is an employee, a $20,000-a-year salesman for my company."

Colombo was variously described as a family man, a perfect gentleman, and a dedicated friend.

The Feds, however, had another opinion of Mr. Colombo. He was, they said, a mob boss and kingpin who controlled numbers rackets, a sports betting ring, had been involved in systematic hijacking, and operated as a fence for stolen goods. They also said that his legitimate businesses were often used to launder his ill-gotten gains.

Colombo began the Civil Rights League in 1970 after his son, Joe, Jr., was arrested and charged with conspiracy to melt silver coins down into more valuable ingots.

"We said there is a conspiracy in this country against all Italian people," Colombo said in a story he wrote for the Gannett Group newspaper chain. After his son's arrest, the elder Colombo organized daily protest marches in front of the FBI offices in Manhattan.

"Right there," he said, "we formed the Italian-American Civil Rights League, right on Sixty-Ninth Street and Third Avenue."

It was a bold move by a man believed to head one of the city's most active gangs.

The League attracted scores of newspaper stories and television broadcasts. Members were attractive newsmakers because they targeted well-knowns like the producers of the *Godfather* films, and won concessions on civil rights matters. In that instance they got the producer to agree to edit out of the movie any references to the Costa Nostra. In another case they persuaded the makers of Alka-Seltzer to stop airing television commercials the League felt slandered Italian-Americans. The one they found particularly distasteful used the words "Mamma mia, thatsa some spicy meatball!"

When Joseph Colombo was shot, he had just faced federal income tax evasion charges and had recently been convicted on perjury charges in connection with obtaining a real estate license. New York officials said Colombo had lied on his application, stating that he had no arrest record. However, authorities said he had been arrested at least thirteen times, with three convictions. In addition, he had recently been implicated in a ten-million-dollar citywide gambling syndicate.

Colombo never fully recovered from the wounds he suffered at that rally in the summer of 1971. The shots to his head had caused considerable brain damage, and for all practical purposes, he was a dead man the instant those bullets struck. He lingered for about seven years, with repeated stays in the hospital, until he died in upstate New York, another victim of a brutal rubout.

Chapter 18
Gone But Not Forgotten:
The Tale of Jimmy Hoffa

In some ways, this was the perfect hit
except that the satisfaction
of seeing the victim was denied both
the press and the mob; on the other
hand, public interest has never faded,
which is not so good, from
the hitter's point-of-view....

THE sudden and complete disappearance of Teamsters
Union boss Jimmy Hoffa, whose middle name ironically was Riddle, ranks among the most classic hits in
the annals of American crime. The story, which began
with a routine missing-persons report filed by Hoffa's
family with the Bloomfield Township, Michigan police
on July 31, 1975, is still cloudy. Whatever happened
to the former president of the International Brotherhood
of Teamsters union remains unknown.

The initial investigation fell to the local cops, who
were aided by the Oakland County Prosecutor's office.
On that first morning, Hoffa's name was logged in
along with hundreds of other missing-persons reports.
The implications of what might have happened and why
were intriguing from the beginning. The cops immediately suspected foul play, but that was based on pure

conjecture, not evidence. All that could be confirmed that morning was the fact that Hoffa, a powerful, outspoken figure, had gone to a restaurant and was never seen again. County Prosecutor L. Brooks Patterson told reporters that all they had were theories. For the time being, they were treating his disappearance as a possible homicide. The possibilities seemed endless. The local union was in turmoil, as evidenced by recent car bombings and the common knowledge that Hoffa, once the national head, meant to regain power.

This led to the not-so-idle speculation that the current leadership, headed by President Frank Fitzsimmons, was somehow involved. Fitzsimmons' son Richard narrowly escaped death a month earlier when his car was blown up in a parking lot. Hoffa and the elder Fitzsimmons were contenders to run the 1.7 million member union.

The police immediately suspected a mob connection after Hoffa's son, James, Jr., told the cops his father had planned a meeting with one Anthony Giacalone, a reputed Mafia figure well known in Detroit. Giacalone, however, was a close friend of the family, not some low-life thug putting the arm on Hoffa for a favor or money. Among other things, Giacalone had been implicated on federal charges in connection with mail fraud, conspiracy, and income tax evasion. The meeting was supposedly planned after the fifty-six-year-old mobster sought Hoffa's advice concerning his upcoming tax trial. That thin thread, however, snapped after it was learned that the two men had met at least two weeks before Hoffa disappeared.

Former Teamsters Vice President Anthony "Tony Pro" Provenzano, who had been living in Fort Lauderdale, Florida, but was still powerful in New Jersey

Teamsters locals, became a suspect when it was learned that he and Hoffa had parted ways after an undisclosed dispute while both served time in Lewisburg Federal Prison. Provenzano, who did time for extortion, was seen in Detroit shortly before Hoffa disappeared and had allegedly threatened Hoffa in front of other union officials. The specific nature of the threat and under what circumstances it was made never came out. Federal agents joined the case, volunteering to track Provenzano down and interview him. It was routine police work, not a manhunt. Union insiders said that Provenzano had publicly supported Hoffa's run for the presidency of the union. The two men, however, severed their friendship after Hoffa refused during his previous tenure as president to amend the union bylaws for the pension fund so that Provenzano could draw his pension when he was released from jail.

Meanwhile, two more unnamed suspects, also alleged to have planned meetings with Hoffa shortly before he disappeared, joined the long list of possible suspects. In the daily papers, the stories were filled with unidentified people who commented on the case from every conceivable perspective. In one instance, "a source close to the family" said an employee of a friend of Hoffa's had identified the two mysterious men the union leader had planned to meet.

"The source said that Mr. Hoffa had mentioned the names to his friend's employee, Elmer Reeves, before he left to meet the men," it was reported. Reeves, who worked for the Airport Service Line, Inc., had already been interviewed by police but could not remember the names of the two men Hoffa was supposed to meet until the family hired a hypnotist. He said Hoffa had stopped at Airport Service to see Louis Linteau, owner of the company and an old friend, before he left for his last meeting. Linteau, who once headed Local 614 of the union, was out to lunch. After chatting with Reeves, Hoffa then left. Later that day, it was learned that Hoffa was also stood up by Giacalone. The sudden mysterious unavailability of his cohorts might have alerted a more suspicious type that something was in the wind. Clearly Hoffa was not Sicilian.

This led to the speculation that Giacalone set up the meeting as a way of luring Hoffa to the restaurant, where he was abducted. Giacalone denied everything. At the same time, Fitzsimmons also knew nothing.

Hoffa himself added his own touch of mystery by confiding to a friend a week before he dropped out of sight that he feared for his life, saying "Something big is going to happen."

Hoffa's prophecy was as unsatisfying and enigmatic as everything else in this almost factless case. The *New York Times* said, "Mr. Hoffa owes his fate, whatever it may be, to his increasingly persistent efforts to restore his lapsed influence over the 2.2 million member union he built almost single-handedly into one of the most potent economic and political forces in America."

One of the earliest beliefs was that Hoffa, knowing his life was in danger, had fled. However, people close to him discounted it, saying "Jimmy didn't know how to run away from a fight."

The FBI fanned out, talking to thousands of people within two weeks of his disappearance, and still could not put together a rational theory to explain what happened to Jimmy Hoffa. The most likely explanation was that he had been abducted and killed. People have been asking why ever since.

Some thought he was done in by Teamsters acting on orders from high-ranking members of the union or by known figures in organized crime circles. Although Teamsters held down solid, working-class jobs like truck drivers, steel workers, and pipefitters, they weren't known as choirboys. There had long been a suspicion that Teamster locals aligned themselves closely with the Mafia for both money and influence. Was Hoffa somehow a threat to this long-standing association?

Politically, it had been rumored that Hoffa was planning to make his run for the presidency of the union in 1976. His family denied it. Hoffa, who had been convicted of jury tampering, was granted a conditional pardon from prison but was prohibited from participating in union activities. At the time of his disappearance, repeated attempts to hammer at the constitutionality of those conditions through court appeals had failed. Until that hurdle was cleared, which it had not been in 1975, Hoffa couldn't run for the presidency without risking a parole violation. Three appeals court judges were hearing the case, but Hoffa couldn't have known how they were going to rule. Nevertheless, it was common knowledge that he wanted to return to power.

Others rumored that Jimmy was planning to repay some bad feelings by testifying before a grand jury looking into insurance and pension fund kickbacks paid to top union officials. It wouldn't be the first time a valuable witness had been done away with. It had been rumored that not only was Hoffa planning to testify himself, he had also been encouraging others to talk before a federal grand jury.

Hoffa, who had a running battle with government officials dating back to 1957 and considered himself a personal enemy of former U.S. Attorney General Robert Kennedy, wasn't a patriotic soul. However, if his opponents in the union election were doing time, their prospects for winning office were dim, to say the least.

In the past, Hoffa had been called before the grand jury, but he had reportedly kept his mouth shut. However, a grand jury in Michigan indicted Giacalone shortly after Hoffa appeared before it, one year before Hoffa's disappearance. Giacalone, known as "Tony Jack," wasn't thrilled by the ensuing events, but no one could swear Hoffa had ratted.

It has long been believed that a feud resulted when Hoffa's was released, even though he was restricted from union activities as a condition of his release. Fitzsimmons was another lively suspect, since he had a lot to gain from Jimmy's absence.

Under Hoffa, all the power in the union lay in his hands. Under Fitzsimmons, that power was delegated to the fifteen international vice presidents. Hoffa ruled with an iron fist, paying surprise visits to local operations, making telephone calls in the middle of the night, barking out orders. Mob figures had gotten used to dealing with the local vice presidents. "Whoever controls the Teamsters," said one government labor expert, "has power, money and an army of truck drivers at his disposal."

According to the speculation, Giacalone might have had a motive if Hoffa did finger him for the grand jury. Fitzsimmons rose to prominence only after Hoffa was jailed. With Jimmy free and making no bones about his ambitions, Fitzsimmons, too, might have wanted Hoffa out of the way. The mob in general had enjoyed years of untethered relationships with the union's locals, something that might come to a halt if Hoffa were back in charge. Many people had ample reason to get Jimmy.

While the authorities scrambled to piece together a scenario from rumor, innuendo, and unrelated facts, they were certain of at least two things: The hit on Jimmy Hoffa was approved by high-ranking mobsters or union officials, and Hoffa did not survive the ordeal.

It was warm and sunny that afternoon in July when James Riddle Hoffa left his two-story summer home forty miles north of Detroit and drove off in his Pontiac. Hoffa told his wife, Josephine, that he was meeting three friends for lunch. By three o'clock he had vanished forever.

After making a few stops, Hoffa arrived at the Red Fox, a restaurant about fifteen miles from downtown Detroit. He was seen in the parking lot between 1:30 and 2:30 P.M. and reportedly appeared to be waiting for someone. Hoffa's lunch companions were late, so he called Josephine and asked if Giacalone had called to cancel. He also called a friend who owned a car service and told him his companions had failed to show up. The last time anyone reported seeing Hoffa was at quarter to three that afternoon. Tony Giacalone, banished to Florida by younger mobsters, had been visiting relatives when Hoffa turned up missing.

Reeves said that Hoffa told him he was meeting Tony Pro and T.J. for lunch. Giacalone was called Tony Jack, T.J. for short.

In an unusual move, Provenzano called a news conference shortly after unofficial allegations were made against him and denied everything. Giacalone, who also told his story to reporters while refusing to talk to federal authorities, said that he, too, had not met with Hoffa the afternoon he disappeared. In fact, Giacalone said, he had spent the day at the Southfield Athletic Club near downtown Detroit, where he'd had a rubdown and a haircut.

Enter Chuckie O'Brien, Hoffa's adopted son. Chuckie was employed by the union in Detroit, earning an estimated $30,000. Making ends meet was difficult because he had to pay child support to his former wife. It was rumored that he had no permanent address, and apparently wasn't popular with the union officials for whom he worked. He had been sent to California for a short time and was slated to be exiled to Alaska. O'Brien had secretly remarried. Hoffa's natural son, James, Jr. and his sister, Barbara Crancer, said their adopted brother knew more about their father's disappearance than he was saying. O'Brien denied it, then he dropped out of sight. He later denied that, too, saying the FBI knew of his whereabouts throughout the investigation. O'Brien said he was with his uncle Tony the afternoon Hoffa was abducted. Early in August, O'Brien said he also traveled to Washington to visit Frank Fitzsimmons, the man his father had vowed to unseat as head of the union. Fitzsimmons said O'Brien sought his advice on how to answer the allegations against him.

Privately, Hoffa family members said that O'Brien joined the Fitzsimmon's camp long before his father disappeared. This, too, was denied by O'Brien. In Bloomfield Hills, when asked to take a lie detector test, however, O'Brien refused. Meanwhile, the FBI impounded a Mercury O'Brien claimed he had borrowed the day his father had disappeared. As part of his alibi, O'Brien said he borrowed the car from a Joseph Giacalone, the son of Anthony Giacalone. He said he had purchased a twenty-pound coho salmon for a union official and, as he was delivering it, the package leaked blood on the carpet of Giacalone's car, so he had it washed. Agents who inspected the car did find bloodstains on the floor—fish blood.

The Hoffa family offered a $200,000 reward to anyone who could help solve the Hoffa mystery. The money was never collected. Exactly seven years later, James Hoffa, Jr. the Teamster's son, petitioned a Detroit court to declare his father legally dead. "It's nearing the end of a long journey of waiting and hoping," he told a reporter. "Of course, at this late date, nobody has any hope." It was 1982. Hoffa's wife, Josephine, had died two years earlier without ever knowing what really happened to her husband.

What happened to Jimmy Hoffa? The prevailing theory is that he was lured to the Red Fox restaurant and was met by someone close to him, an unwitting accomplice to thugs who knocked Hoffa unconscious and dragged his body off to an incinerator, where the body was burned and disposed of without a trace. Even that story, served up by a news weekly shortly after the courts officially declared Hoffa dead, was mere speculation.

Chapter 19
Lie Down with Dogs:
Allen Dorfman

As crime and ordinary business increasingly overlapped, more and more transitional figures like Dorfman surfaced ... and died. Associates of "made" men are not very valuable because they are not really family. They are not Amici Nostri.

ALLEN M. Dorfman, a brash smoothy who some said became too smart for his own good, earned the dubious distinction of becoming number 1,081 in a long list of gangland murders committed since 1919. He got it in January, 1983, abruptly ending decades of almost unspoiled wealth and influence through mob and union connections. When the end came in a parking lot outside a suburban Chicago hotel, the killing was a textbook classic, carried out with precision by professional hit men who stalked their prey, then struck with lightning speed. It was apparently carried out to silence Dorfman's voice in a federal probe into organized crime attempts to rob millions in union pension funds. Dorfman could have told it all.

Dorfman, once a close friend of Jimmy Hoffa, had been accused by federal investigators of having a hand in delivering to the mob millions in pension funds belonging to the International Brotherhood of Teamsters. As he strolled across a parking lot at the Hyatt Lincolnwood Hotel just outside of Chicago with his associate Irwin Weiner, two men wearing ski masks approached from behind. The men announced a holdup and one of them pulled out a gun, firing at close range into his head. The two men ignored a stunned Weiner and fled in a green car.

Millionaire Dorfman, wearing an expensive brown camel hair coat, lay dead on the ground. His wallet and other valuables remained on his body. The only thing lost was the life of a man long suspected to have mob connections, and who probably knew too much.

One investigating officer at the scene told a news magazine reporter that few who knew Dorfman would be surprised when they got the news. "Close association with the Cosa Nostra often leads to sudden death," he said. Long before a single shot was fired, authorities had been saying that Allan Dorfman's lights would soon be put out.

Officially, Dorfman emerged as a leading figure in union business back in 1949 when he was befriended by Hoffa, then an ambitious union leader in Detroit.

As Jimmy rose in the union, Dorfman cashed in, too, selling insurance to the union's Central States Health and Welfare Fund. According to a *Time* magazine story, Dorfman doubled as Hoffa's powerful lieutenant in union affairs. When Hoffa was indicted and convicted on perjury charges, he made it clear that Dorfman's position in union affairs would remain secure. Along the way, Dorfman and members of his family surfaced periodically in connection with various wrongdoings, including unearned commissions through the insurance agency they owned.

In 1953, for example, Dorfman and his wife, Rose, were hauled before a congressional committee investigating insurance fraud in Detroit. Investigators of the House Labor and Education Subcommittee believed that, in one instance, the Dorfmans received more than $100,000 in unearned commissions from the A.F.L. union over a four-year period. It was believed to be just part of millions of dollars milked from the union through Dorfman's connections.

When called to testify, the one-time boxer refused to talk. Hoffa was a suspect in the investigation, although his role was not clearly brought out during the 1953 hearings.

Allen and Rose Dorfman owned the Union Insurance Agency of Illinois. Investigators said that the company was paid at least $1,142,000.00 in commissions from Chicago Local 1031, the Teamsters' Central States Health and Welfare Fund, and the Michigan Conference of Teamsters, beginning in January 1950. Hoffa and others were charged with receiving kickbacks for these payments, although strong evidence linking Hoffa to the scheme failed to materialize.

Dorfman's refusal to testify during the hearings got him cited for contempt. He then got nailed in 1972 for accepting a $55,000 kickback on a dubious pension fund loan, and did nine months time. When Jimmy disappeared forever one afternoon in 1975, Dorfman continued to control billions in loan deals with organized crime, according to authorities.

Dorfman also owned Amalgamated Insurance Agency, Inc., which took in the premiums and processed claims made through Teamsters policies. The

Feds, investigating links between Amalgamated and mobsters, said Dorfman was at least in part responsible for siphoning more than five million dollars from the union's pension fund. In fact, many close to the investigation said that Dorfman was really the power behind the union after he successfully ousted Frank Fitzsimmons, who took over after Hoffa's demise.

Under Dorfman, the union made questionable loans to companies owning gambling interests in Las Vegas. *Newsweek* quoted investigators who credited Dorfman with knowing about "murders . . . offshore money washing" and the "connections with every Mafioso and every Mafia lawyer in the country. He knew it all."

Eight years later, his intimate knowledge of who got what and when, cost him everything. Dorfman had been convicted the month before his death of bribing U.S. Senator Howard Cannon of Nevada. Many, including mob insiders, smelled a deal between the affable Dorfman and federal investigators. He faced a maximum of fifty-five years in jail on his conviction, unless he could barter with prosecutors anxious to get more than a roof-top view of union activities. At sixty years old, the conviction meant dying in jail, unless he could make a deal.

After the killing, reporters swarmed to the scene. The area was roped off and investigators dusted the area for clues. There were none; just eyewitnesses who had seen the shooting.

"A lot of people will sleep better tonight knowing that Dorfman is silenced," Patrick F. Healy, head of the Chicago Crime Commission, said to a news magazine reporter.

Chapter 20
Paul Castellano

WHEN the Feds nabbed reputed Mafia chieftain Paul Castellano, once head of the largest organized crime family in America, prosecutors trying to put him away for murder-conspiracy and operating a car theft ring couldn't have known their case against him would be interrupted by an occupational hazard—death.

Castellano, don of the Gambino family, was gunned down on a Manhattan street in December of 1985, three months after he and nine other defendants went on trial in Federal Court. The seventy-year-old Don and his underworld associate, Thomas Bilotti, were hit by three assassins armed with semiautomatic weapons as horrified onlookers watched.

Shortly before 5:30 that evening, Bilotti drove Castellano to Sparks Steak House at 210 East Forty-Sixth Street and parked close to the restaurant near Third Avenue. Castellano occasionally went to Sparks but had no reservation that night. It was December 17, a frosty night, and the street was filled with holiday shoppers laden down with shopping bags and gaily wrapped parcels. When Castellano opened the passenger door of the car, witnesses told police that three men in trench coats approached and began firing. As shoppers ran away screaming, the gunmen pumped six shots into each man. Bilotti fell in the street, lying face up. Castellano fell face up, too, his bloodied head resting on the car seat, his body sprawled full-length on the sidewalk.

Ten days earlier, Aniello Dellacroce, the number-two man in the Gambino organization, died at the age of seventy-one. The killing of Castellano and the untimely death of his second-in-command sparked speculation by law enforcement authorities that a long-standing rift among Gambino factions had widened. Paul Castellano's surprise death suggested disaffection among the rank and file. It looked like an internal struggle was underway to take control of the family, believed to be the largest and most powerful crime organization in the United States.

Even in death Paul Castellano could not rest in peace. On December 19, two days after his shooting, John Cardinal O'Connor of the New York Archdiocese refused to allow a public funeral mass for Castellano. The Reverend Peter Finn, a spokesman, said that a public mass was banned because of Castellano's "notoriety." He was buried at the Moravian Cemetery in West Brighton on Staten Island. A priest was present at the burial in a Protestant cemetery. The church did allow Castellano's family to conduct a private memorial service at the Blessed Sacrament Roman Catholic Church, but the body was not allowed to be present.

"This could be the beginning of a major mob war," said one official of the Organized Crime Strike Force of the United States Justice Department, after the Castellano/Bilotti hit.

Castellano was the brother-in-law of Carlo Gambino, who was bumped off by Mother Nature in 1976. Castellano assumed power in a bloodless takeover from Dellacroce when Gambino died. Dellacroce quietly accepted the number-two spot, but federal authorities said that tension between soldiers loyal to Dellacroce and those who followed Castellano remained high. The Dellacroce group was more prone to violence, while the Castellano group had concentrated on white-collar crimes and labor racketeering.

U.S. Attorney Rudolph Giuliani expressed outrage over the killings of Castellano and Bilotti. The slayings cheated the ambitious prosecutor of what might have been one of the most stunning victories against organized crime. If Castellano and Bilotti had not been killed, Giuliani might have successfully prosecuted them.

Giuliani was quoted as saying, "Law enforcement has an obligation to investigate fully and to try and identify and prosecute those people who are responsible for the shootings. A murder makes the whole world a little bit less safe for everybody—no matter who is murdered."

As late as December 1989, no witnesses had come forward, although police said that at least two witnesses had been close enough to the gunmen to possibly identify them.

In an *America's Most Wanted* broadcast, the host of the show said, "The three gunmen vanished . . . in a Lincoln Town Car. The key to this case might be in your hands. When the shooting occurred, two women might have gotten a close look at the killers. One woman rushed to the side of the forty-five-year-old Bilotti and appeared to take his pulse.'' The broadcaster said police believed she might have been a nurse. The other woman was on the sidewalk near the side of the car where Castellano was shot. She, too, might have seen his killers.

Police said the Gambino organization had nearly a thousand members, two hundred fifty of which had taken an oath of secrecy. They are believed to have been involved in a variety of rackets, including gambling, loan-sharking, hijacking, labor-racketeering, and drug-trafficking in New York, Pennsylvania, New Jersey, Nevada, and Florida. At the time of his death, Castellano was free on two million dollars bond.

The animosity between the Castellano factions and those loyal to Dellacroce was revealed in wiretap information obtained by federal officials. They said the Dellacroce crew was concerned that when Dellacroce died, Castellano might attempt to turn over the reins of the organization to one of his own people. If Castellano was convicted on the murder-conspiracy charge, the same thing might happen, which probably prompted them to whack him before a successor could be named.

Even though he had been blessed by the mighty Don Carlo himself, it was felt that Castellano had never achieved the level of authority and respect Gambino had effortlessly maintained.

He ''never attained the rank of boss of bosses within the underworld,'' authorities said. ''FBI agents said the unwritten code of the Mafia would permit the murder of a boss for only three reasons: if he had become a government informer; if he had breached a rule within the Mafia, such as having an affair with another member's wife; or as part of a larger power struggle.'' It was this third reason authorities believe prompted Castellano's assassination.

In 1985, the Mafia came under increasing pressure from law enforcement authorities. Indictments came down against the leaders of the five major U.S. organized crime families. According to a 1983 New York Police Department estimate, the Gambino group had two hundred fifty "made" or full-fledged members and hundreds of "associates." That family was ruled by Carlo Gambino, the so-called "Boss of All Bosses" from at least 1957 until his death in the late 1970s.

Some officials believed that Dellacroce was really the head of that family, although Castellano was called boss. The other families were identified as the Joseph Bonanno group, the Joseph Colombo crew, the Luchese faction, and the Vito Genovese boys.

Each family was named for its founder, even when the founders were either long-dead or retired. Joseph Bonanno retired in the 1950s after fleeing to Canada to escape assassination. In 1985, that group was headed by Philip Rastelli, a co-defendant in the Castellano murder trial. The Colombo family was headed by Genaro Langello, sometimes known as Gerry Lang, also a co-defendant in the Castellano trial. The Luchese crime family was headed by Anthony Corallo. Two high-ranking members of that family—Salvatore Santoro, underboss, and *consigliere* Christopher Furnari, were also co-defendants in the Catellano case.

The Genovese family at the time was headed by Anthony Salerno, who took over when Vito Genovese died in 1969 of natural causes.

The name John Gotti emerged after the Castellano killing as the heir apparent to the Gambino crime family. "John Gotti, a fastidious, well-groomed forty-five-year-old resident of Queens, is believed by law enforcement officials to be a central figure in an internal fight for leadership of the Gambino crime family,'' according to news accounts at the time. ''John Gotti is a major organized crime figure,'' *The New York Times* said, quoting a high-ranking police official. ''Gotti will emerge as the head of the other *capos*—that's what this struggle is all about,'' the newspaper said. ''Bilotti was Gotti's rival, and he's gone, and there may well be some more killings before it's settled.''

Like many of his predecessors, Castellano had the demeanor of a successful meat salesman rather than a mob boss. He lived quietly in a Staten Island mansion, away from the glitter of Manhattan nightlife. Authorities say Castellano may have been caught between the old-world–style mob bosses and an emerging need to enjoy the status of being a legitimate businessman. By 1985, the Mafia had successfully hooked into many different businesses. They were fully entrenched in a number of powerful unions and operated catering businesses and refuse carting operations throughout New York, New Jersey and Pennsylvania.

''The crime group that Mr. Castellano and nine other men were accused of operating purportedly committed twenty-five murders to eliminate witnesses and competitors, among other crimes,'' one newspaper account said after his death. ''Yet Mr. Castellano was said to have been personally repelled by excessive brutality. Only two weeks ago, a witness testified that Mr. Castellano had expressed disgust because members of a car-theft ring, in killing a suspected police informant, had also murdered the man's nineteen-year-old girlfriend. Mr. Castellano wanted to know why the girl was killed,'' one of the witnesses testified. In fact, even his prosecutors had relatively kind words for the man they were trying to convict.

"There will be no evidence that he shot anyone or stole any cars," said federal prosecutor Walter S. Mack, Jr. "He was the president; he had to oversee the operation."

The legitimacy of the Castellano meat business emerged during the trial when it was revealed that his company, Meat Palace, in the Bay Ridge section of Brooklyn, was the distributor of Perdue Chickens. He was said to have met with chicken king Frank Perdue on at least one occasion during a 1981 union organizing campaign at a Perdue processing plant in Virginia. The director of a major task force on organized crime said that the Castellano killing had been approved by the chief Mafia bosses in New York.

Ronald Goldstock, director of the State Organized Crime Task Force, said that leaders of the Colombo, Luchese, Bonanno, and Genovese crime families had approved the hit "because his legal and internal organization problems were endangering all of them. Castellano was an important person, and I believe his assassination had to be approved by the other leaders," Goldstock said in an interview with the *New York Times*. "There was a possibility he could take all of them down," the investigator said. It was Goldstock's office that played a key role in the Castellano indictment that also hauled in nine other high-powered Mafia figures.

Goldstock outlined the elements which eventually led to the decision to take Castellano out before further damage could be done to mob figures implicated along with him:

The dispute between the Castellano and Della-croce factions.

The belief that Castellano was neglecting the business affairs of the Gambino family because of his legal difficulties.

In addition to the murder-conspiracy charges, he also faced five other state and federal indictments.

The various mob bosses worried that Castellano was becoming careless, and had done nothing to avoid being indicted. They cited as evidence the fact that federal agents had been able to success-fully bug his Staten Island home.

Castellano could not meet with various crime family leaders because he was under constant sur-veillance. He couldn't authorize new ventures or run earlier business ventures because he was being watched so closely. "He was costing them their livelihoods," Goldstock said.

Goldstock's evaluation was mirrored by the opinion of G. Robert Blakey, a University of Notre Dame law professor, who has served as a consultant on organized crime to congressional panels investigating mob activities.

He said the hit was "almost certainly approved by top leaders in his own family and the commission. My guess is there is not going to be a mob war," he went on, but added that the "Gotti faction" is more prone to violence than Castellano had been during his tenure. He said that a campaign by authorities on the local, state, and federal levels to disrupt the activities of the five crime families contributed to the decision to kill Castellano. "Absent these trials and the pressure produced by them, Castellano would still be alive," the professor said.

The mob, however, might have overestimated the government's ability to win a conviction. The prosecution attempted to link Castellano to twenty-five murders and a stolen-car ring. However, newspaper accounts characterized the trial as a series of "missteps by the prosecution." Witnesses in a number of instances either misidentified defendants or could not identify them at all.

U.S. District Court Judge Kevin Thomas Duffy repeatedly criticized the U.S. Attorney's office for showing up in court unprepared. The jury was treated to some impressive police work when the prosecution was able to trace numerous transactions involving stolen cars. On one occasion the prosecution showed how at least two defendants had been involved in the theft of hundreds of cars eventually shipped to Kuwait. Several of the cars were recovered. But when FBI agents testified in connection with that evidence, they could not identify one of the defendants, marring the prosecution's case.

The trial continued for about ten weeks before any witnesses could link Castellano to the car ring. That witness, Dominick Montiglio, said he delivered money obtained from selling the stolen cars directly to Castellano. He also testified to Castellano's displeasure with the killings associated with the car ring. A short time later, however, Montiglio's testimony was questioned when he admitted to lying before the grand jury.

Former U.S. Attorney Michael Mukasey, a one-time colleague of Giuliani, jumped to his defense in a newspaper opinion story printed during the Castellano trial, just a few weeks before the Castellano murder.

"The Mafia exists," Mukasey said. "It is not the creation of novelists or journalists. It has exacted a toll in misery that would shame the Inquisition, and a toll in treasure that would embarrass the Pentagon. It consists not of dashing Robin Hoods or buffoons, but of willful, disciplined men who have too long burdened all of us.

"Against this private army, law enforcement recently has made unprecedented inroads. The leaders of the five major families in New York are under indictment, including not only the top five but also one hundred thirty associates and lieutenants.

"Yet, United States Attorney Rudolph W. Giuliani . . . has been unfairly charged with violating ethical rules by supposedly disclosing improper information at news conferences, with threatening the presumption of innocence by indicting defendants under their *noms de guerre* (for example, Frank 'the Beast' Falanga), with jailing without bail; with conducting mass trials; with wrongfully subpoenaing defense lawyers and picking jurors anonymously—a one-man war on the Constitution if you take these charges at face value."

Mukasey said that Giuliani acted properly in explaining the indictments at press conferences where he stuck "strictly to matters already in the public record. After all, the public is entitled to know about the Mafia," Mukasey said. He said the indictments used the aliases, "to make testimony and tape recordings comprehensible to juries." The mass trials violated no judicial codes either. "Those charged with acting criminally together may be tried together."

Montiglio's testimony was significant because authorities believed he had painted an accurate picture of mob activities in the late 1980s. He said that he had been a collector in the Gambino family for loan-sharking activities, and a go-between in large drug deals. A Vietnam veteran, Montiglio said he was able to boobytrap cars so they would explode when the ignition was turned on.

In court papers, Montiglio said that an extortion racket began with the visit of several soldiers to a bar or night club, where they would start a fight or cause some sort of disturbance. Later, he said, gang members would make it known to the owners that this sort of thing would happen more and more.

"Then I would get together with the owner and I would say I could probably straighten that out" if the owner agreed to make regular payments to collectors like himself, Montiglio testified.

Montiglio was admitted to the federal witness protection program, and had already pleaded guilty to various charges when he testified. That admission cast a doubtful light on all he had said earlier in the trial.

Dellacroce, nicknamed Neil, had been hospitalized two weeks before his death, registering at Mary Immaculate Hospital in Queens under the name of Timothy O'Neil. He had been indicted on federal racketeering charges, and faced prosecution for evading taxes and participating in a ruling "commission of organized crime." Those charges were separate from those handed down against Castellano.

Authorites said that Dellacroce was in charge of Manhattan operations for the Gambino clan. He was known to operate out of 247 Mulberry Street, lower Manhattan, in a place known as the Ravenite Social Club. He was arrested there by IRS agents in 1984 on tax evasion charges after law enforcement officers had successfully wiretapped the club four years earlier.

Those wiretaps revealed discussions concerning the 1979 murder of Mafia chieftain Carmine Galante.

ON the stand, Montiglio recreated conversations he said he overheard involving Castellano. One of them referred to the murder of John Quinn, a rival car thief killed in 1977, and Quinn's girlfriend, Cherie Golden. These murders were two of five killings prosecutors attempted to tie to the car-theft ring. Montiglio said he was privy to conversations between Castellano and his uncle Anthony Gaggi, a lieutenant in the Gambino organization. "My uncle was a little perturbed about the girl getting killed," he testified. "Mr. Castellano asked my uncle why this girl Cherie was killed. My uncle told him she was part of the operation with Quinn, and something about him going to the law and he had to be taken care of." Under cross-examination by defense lawyers, Montiglio said he had not told "the whole truth" to federal agents after being questioned for more than two hundred hours. He did not come forward until a week before the trial began in October of 1985.

"Don't you know, sir, that you never mentioned any one of those things you said to Mr. Castellano until September 23, 1985?" defense attorney James LaRossa said, discrediting the witness. "And you are telling us that notwithstanding the fact that you spent two hundred-plus hours with agents and a full day in the grand jury, you chose to perjure yourself," LaRossa said.

"Yes," Montiglio said. "At the time, I wasn't telling the whole truth."

A week after he was killed, law enforcement intelligence reports showed that it may have been Bilotti who was the target of the hit, not his boss, Castellano. It was an attempt to block Bilotti's rise to the throne in the event that Castellano was sentenced to jail or killed.

Shortly after the murders, authorities said that a group led by John Gotti had been seen meeting in Queens and in lower Manhattan with Castellano soldiers. They met at least once in Ozone Park at the Bergen Hunt and Fish Club in Queens, and at the Ravenite Social Club on Mulberry Street. Police said the meetings were called to smooth over their differences and to decide who would succeed Castellano. The intelligence reports named possible rivals who might challenge Gotti. These included Joseph Gallo, the seventy-four-year-old *consigliere,* and James Failla, a member of the Dellacroce faction.

Throughout the investigation, high-ranking officials suspected that Gotti was behind Castellano's murder. "After reviewing information gleaned mainly from stool pigeons and spy devices, investigators believed that the Gotti boys had marked Bilotti as an equal target with Mr. Castellano to prevent him from fighting for control of the entire family."

Bilotti had become Castellano's chief aide, and there had been a long-standing dispute between Bilotti and Gotti. Bilotti was known as a tough enforcer within the Gambino family. "Mr. Bilotti had a reputation . . . as one of the toughest leaders in the Castellano faction and had been known to smash opponents over the head with a baseball bat to end disputes," reports the New York Times.

When asked to appear for questioning, an attorney for Gotti said his client would not cooperate. "My client has no information, no comment and knows nothing about the murders."

*   *   *

THE government had begun a systematic, coordinated assault on organized crime. At the same time Castellano was on trial, authorities were also trying to lock up several other high-ranking mob figures.

Several members of the Joseph Colombo crime family were on trial on racketeering charges. Carmine Persico and ten other family members were on trial in federal court. While old-line mobsters were being tried for murder, extortion, and other typical crimes, a new breed of mob figures began to appear in court. Gone were the pin-striped suits and fedora hats. Gone was the broken English and threats of violence. In their place the sons of long-time gangsters showed up in court dressed as suave businessmen, armed with expert legal counsel and sophisticated strategies.

One example was the trial of reputed mob figure Michael Franzese of Brookville, Long Island, who went on trial for conspiracy to defraud businesses and the government through extortion, false credit cards, and the use of dummy corporations. (Franzese was indicted in December of 1985 on racketeering charges.)

Franzese was said to own at least eighteen companies which served as fronts for his alleged illegal activities. In contrast to Castellano, Franzese was characterized by his lawyer as "good-looking, bright, articulate."

"This is not the 'pizza case,' with two million dollars in heroin, not the Castellano case with twenty-five murders," said attorney John Jacobs. This is "not your typical Mafioso type." Franzese was the son of John Franzese, a long-time Mafia figure. "I think he's a victim of a vendetta by the government because of his father," said Jacobs, himself a former Organized Crime Task Force prosecutor. "They believe he's taken over for his father."

Authorities said that the younger Franzese was just old wine in a new bottle. They argued that his crimes were more elaborate versions of the bank jobs his father was reputed to have organized and pulled off.

"If people you're going to do business with think you're a member of a Mafia syndicate they're much more likely to do business with you on your terms," a professor at Pennsylvania State University was quoted as saying in the *New York Times* about Franzese. "It may well be that Michael Franzese has benefited from his father's reputation and the mythology surrounding the Mafia." The indictment against Franzese said the "group operated a criminal enterprise not through common street crimes but through fraudulent schemes for which they infiltrated some of the country's most respected and established industries and businesses."

IN August of 1985, a federal grand jury indicted more than twenty-five people accused of being members of the Luchese crime family. They were described as "young, aggressive, intelligent and sophisticated people in their thirties who lived in half-million dollar homes and drove expensive cars." Authorities said that this new breed of mobsters had broken their ties with the old-line Mafia and their old-world approach to organized crime.

Chapter 21
Your Hit Parade—1990

The lyrics are different, but it's the same old tune.

HAS the world of organized crime changed in the past sixty years? Yes, one might say. The streets of Chicago are no longer littered with gangsters' dead bodies. But is that all that's different now?

In the 1972 film *The Godfather*, Michael Corleone, heir to his father's criminal empire, tells Kay Adams that "if everything goes right, the Corleone family will be completely legitimate in five years."

As every moviegoer knows, it doesn't happen. What does happen is that the Corleones take on a *semblance* of legitimacy. They move to Nevada and openly operate legal gambling casinos, while covertly involving themselves in racketeering, prostitution, narcotics, and any other illicit market they can corner. Life imitates art in that respect. Today, mobsters are realtors or restauranteurs, but behind the scenes, as with Michael Corleone, it's business as usual.

A textbook example of the contemporary "goodfellow" is John Gotti. Perfectly barbered, wearing fifteen-hundred-dollar suits and three-hundred-dollar shoes, he's become a media darling, the subject of articles in *People, Vanity Fair, Time* and *Newsweek*. His comings and goings are chronicled on TV magazine shows nearly as much as those of Madonna and Tom Cruise. And Gotti is always smiling, which is hardly surprising. From the humblest of beginnings he has risen to a top position in organized crime, and has been called "Capo di Tutti Capi," crimeland's "Boss of all Bosses," though the position is more a media invention than a real job.

John Joseph Gotti was born to Italian immigrant parents in 1940, the fifth of thirteen children. He grew up in Brooklyn, a "tough guy" who quit school at sixteen. As a youngster he was a member of the Fulton Rockaway Boys, participating in street rumbles that might have inspired those in *West Side Story*. When he grew a little older he worked for a short time in a garment factory as a coat presser. He was married at age twenty, and within three years fathered three children, two boys and a girl.

Despite this prosaic background, Gotti always lived on the edge. During the 1960s he was jailed several times for burglaries. In 1973 he allegedly committed murder for his boss, Carlo Gambino, who hired attorney Roy Cohn to spring him after his arrest.

At about this same time, Gotti bought a house in Howard Beach, Queens. Shortly thereafter, his twelve-year-old son Frank was hit by a car and killed. The driver of the car was a neighbor of Gotti's named John Folaria. Not too long after the fatal accident, Folaria was kidnapped in front of the Castro Convertibles store where he worked, and was never seen again.

Rumors abounded following the kidnapping. Folklore

has it that Folaria went the way of Jimmy Hoffa, and was probably buried six feet under in the New Jersey Meadowlands. When you consider the petty cases the government keeps trying to nail Gotti with, if they had anything at all on Folaria, the government would have looked to indict Gotti.

Considering that Gotti's hero was Albert Anastasia, also known as "The Executioner," it's no wonder that such rumors would arise. Like his idol, John Gotti was ambitious. He rose through the ranks of the Gambino crime family and, after Gambino's death, when Paul Castellano became the new don, Gotti simply bided his time, reputedly ordered a hit on Castellano, then placed the fallen crown on his own head.

Also like Anastasia, who faced five murder raps and beat them all, Gotti invariably eludes the grip of the law. In 1987 he was acquitted on all counts of a federal racketeering charge. As recently as July 1990, the FBI announced that it had a "mother lode" of new evidence, including secret tapes that would link Gotti to Paul Catellano's murder. Bruce Cutler, Gotti's attorney, merely laughed when he heard about the new evidence. "Let them produce it," he said confidently. "My client is innocent."

In the meantime, John Gotti tended to his legitimate business, the Arc Plumbing Company in Ozone Park, New York. He drove around town in his Mercedes or Lincoln, ate dinner at his favorite haunt, the Altadonna Restaurant, and continued to throw an annual Fourth of July bash for his friends and neighbors, complete with food and fireworks.

His neighbors still love him. When questioned by newsmen, they sing his praises and pointedly ignore questions about his underworld activities. Vito Boliterri, his barber, is one of his greatest admirers. "Mr. Gotti got a raw deal," he was quoted as saying on *Inside Edition*. "He never did anything that everybody accuses him of."

He never did anything. How familiar that sounds. Meyer Lansky was "just a respectable businessman." Vito Genovese, when convicted on a narcotics charge, said, "They gave me a bum rap." From Dutch Shultz and Legs Diamond to Joey Gallo and Frank Costello, nobody ever did anything illegal. Maybe Joseph Colombo was right: There *is* no Mafia.

In any case, Gotti now faces trial for the Castellano hit. Betting on his conviction, given his past record in court, is a long shot . . .

JAMES ELLROY

"Echoes the Best of Wambaugh"
New York Sunday News

BROWN'S REQUIEM 78741-5/$3.95 US $4.95 Can
Join ex-cop and sometimes P.I. Fritz Brown beneath the
golden glitter of Tinsel Town...where arson, pay-offs, and
porn are all part of the game.

CLANDESTINE 81141-3/$3.95 US/$4.95 Can
Nominated for an Edgar Award for Best Original Paperback
Mystery Novel. A compelling thriller about an ambitious
L.A. patrolman caught up in the sex and sleaze of smog city
where murder is the dark side of love.

KILLER ON THE ROAD 89934-5/$3.95 US/$4.95 Can
Enter the horrifying world of a killer whose bloody trail of
carnage baffles police from coast to coast and whose only
pleasure is to kill...and kill again.

Featuring Lloyd Hopkins

BLOOD ON THE MOON 69851-X/$3.95 US/$4.95 Can
Lloyd Hopkins is an L.A. cop. Hard, driven, brilliant, he's
the man they call in when a murder case looks bad.

BECAUSE THE NIGHT 70063-8/$3.95 US/$4.95 Can
Detective Sergeant Lloyd Hopkins had a hunch that there
was a connection between three bloody bodies and one
missing cop...a hunch that would take him to the dark heart
of madness...and beyond.

GRITTY, SUSPENSEFUL NOVELS
BY MASTER STORYTELLERS
FROM AVON BOOKS

OUT ON THE CUTTING EDGE
by Lawrence Block
70993-7/$4.95 US/$5.95 Can

"Exceptional...A whale of a knockout punch to the solar plexus."
New York Daily News

FORCE OF NATURE
by Stephen Solomita
70949-X/$4.95 US/$5.95 Can

"Powerful and relentlessly engaging...Tension at a riveting peak" *Publishers Weekly*

A TWIST OF THE KNIFE
by Stephen Solomita
70997-X/$4.95 US/$5.95 Can

"A sizzler...Wambaugh and Caunitz had better look out"
Associated Press

BLACK CHERRY BLUES
by James Lee Burke
71204-0/$4.95 US/$5.95 Can

"Remarkable...A terrific story...The plot crackles with events and suspense...Not to be missed!"

Los Angeles Times Book Review